THE
HISPANIC
ELDERLY

A Research
Reference Guide

**Rosina M. Becerra, Ph.D.
David Shaw, M.A.**

UNIVERSITY
PRESS OF
AMERICA

LANHAM • NEW YORK • LONDON

Copyright © 1984 by

University Press of America,™ Inc.

4720 Boston Way
Lanham, MD 20706

3 Henrietta Street
London WC2E 8LU England

Library of Congress Cataloging in Publication Data

Becerra, Rosina M.
    The Hispanic elderly.

    Bibliography: p.
    1. Gerontology literature–United States. 2. Hispanic
American aged. 3. Hispanic American aged–Research. 4.
Hispanic American aged–Bibliography. I. Shaw, David,
M.A. II. Title.
HQ1064.U5B25   1984   305.2'6'072   83–21659
ISBN 0–8191–3626–3 (alk. paper)
ISBN 0–8191–3627–1 (pbk. : alk. paper)

All University Press of America books are produced on acid-free
paper which exceeds the minimum standards set by the National
Historical Publications and Records Commission.

ACKNOWLEDGEMENTS

It is not possible to thank individually all those who helped us compile, evaluate, and summarize the research instruments on which this report is based: the busy professionals who took time to respond to our requests for their instruments and additional information, the members of the expert panel who aided in the evaluation, the members of the community panel who participated in the evaluation, the staff who worked with us, and most especially the Executive Director and Senior Services Director of the International Institute of Los Angeles, John Phalen and Alex Salazar.

At each step of the way, many people helped us at one or more tasks with their personal and professional talents and wisdom. The following people worked directly on many facets of the project: Greg Castillo, Betty Gardner, Larry Larsen, Bonnie Sisson and Richard Verdugo.

Our particular thanks go to our secretary, Judy Dominquez, who provided continuity throughout the project.

The entire project was supported through a grant (#90-AR-0003/01) from the Administration on Aging. Theron Fuller served as project officer.

Rosina M. Becerra

David Shaw

TABLE OF CONTENTS

INTRODUCTION

Research focusing on the elderly has been launched in the past decade to enable policymakers, program developers, and service providers to assess the state of well-being of this growing population. As part of that effort, target groups within the aged cohort have been singled out for specific attention. Among these groups, the Hispanic elderly have either been the central focus of investigation or have been included as a subsample of larger investigations of the population at large or of larger groupings of the elderly.

Information is not easily identified concerning the types of Spanish language instruments that were used for gathering data in these investigations. In addition, the method used in the conduct of research on the Spanish-speaking elderly vary among researchers. Therefore, it becomes difficult to assess systematically the needs of the Spanish-speaking elderly and to develop programs responsive to their special cultural and situational characteristics.

For researchers interested in the Hispanic population, the present guide offers a source of Spanish-language research instruments which have been, or are now being used to assess the Hispanic elderly. Moreover, the guide also considers the knowledge gained from research among the Hispanic elderly and Hispanics in general. Thus, this guide should serve as a starting point from which new research can be designed and conducted.

CHAPTER I

THE ELDERLY HISPANIC: DEMOGRAPHY,
SOCIAL AND PSYCHOLOGICAL FACTORS,
NEEDS, AND PERCEPTIONS

To identify conceptual problems which affect the design of research on Hispanic elders, the authors prepared a comprehensive review of the literature to outline what researchers have found to date. This information provides some insight into the significance of research on Hispanic elders, and serves as a reference point for identifying gaps in existing knowledge of both the size and characteristics of the elderly Hispanic population. To clarify the special needs, experiences, and concerns of elderly Hispanics of all national origins or descents, Chapter I surveys information and statistics on a wide variety of demographic and sociocultural topics.

A. DEMOGRAPHY

The 1980 census count of Hispanics residing in the United States[1] is 14 million, accounting for approximately seven percent of the population. The largest group is of Mexican origin, followed by persons of Puerto Rican origin, and then by persons of Cuban origin. Central Americans, South Americans, and persons of other Spanish origin account for the smallest proportion of Hispanics currently in the U.S.

Almost 87 percent of the Mexican Americans who live in the United States reside in five Southwestern states: Arizona, California, Colorado, New Mexico, and Texas (U.S. Census, 1978). Over half of the total U.S. Hispanic population, mostly Mexican Americans, reside in Texas and California, 30 percent in California and 22 percent in Texas.

According to the 1980 census, Hispanics constitute a majority of the population of San Antonio, Texas. In Los Angeles County, Hispanics constitute 27 percent of the total population, making them the largest ethnic minority group in this area and in New York, San Diego, Phoenix, San Francisco and Denver, Hispanics outnumber Blacks.[2]

Age:

According to the 1978 census update, as a group, Hispanic-Americans are relatively young. Persons 55 and over account for about 10 percent of this population, whereas 22 percent of non-Hispanics fall in this age

---

[1]U.S., as defined by the Bureau of the Census, refers to the 50 states, and does not include territories such as Puerto Rico.

[2]Preliminary 1980 data from the Bureau of the Census.

1

group. Representation of older Hispanic people varies considerably according to national origin. Almost 10 percent of all Cubans belong to the 55-64 age cohort, compared with only 5 percent of Puerto Ricans and 5 percent of Mexican Americans. Even so, the percentage of elderly in the Cuban population is still smaller than the percentage of elderly in the non-Hispanic group.

When older age cohorts are surveyed, these discrepancies become even more pronounced. While only 1.6 percent of the U.S. Puerto Rican population and 2.5 percent of Mexican Americans are in the age group 65-74, 9.1 percent of the Cuban Americans are 65 or older. These figures drop to 0.6 percent for Puerto Ricans, 1.2 percent for Mexican Americans, and 4.2 percent for Cubans in the "old-old", 75+ age group. This compares with a 4 percent representation for 75+ non-Hispanic residents of the U.S.

When combined, these statistics indicate that only 2.2 percent and 3.7 percent respectively, of Puerto Rican and Mexican Americans are 65 years of age of older, while a significantly larger 13.3 percent of the American Cuban population is over 65 years.

What might account for these differences among the Hispanic groups? Moore (1970) and Cantor (1976) point out a number of factors. First, many Mexican Americans and Puerto Ricans return to their homelands in their late years while many Cuban Americans are political refugees and remain in the U.S. Secondly, the differences in socioeconomic status between Cuban Americans and the other two groups may result in differences in living conditions and health problems, which may, in turn, shorten life expectancies.

Among most populations, women outlive men, and this is the case among both U.S. Hispanics and non-Hispanics. There are 79 non-Hispanic males aged 55 or over who live in the U.S. for every 100 older non-Hispanic females in the same age group. A similar sex ratio applies for elderly Cuban Americans, 80 men for every 100 women, but the ratio drops dramatically among Puerto Ricans: 67 males over 55 for every 100 females of similar age. In direct contrast to the scarcity of males among older Puerto Ricans, Mexican American women only slightly outnumber their 55+ male peers: 94 males for every 100 females. This ratio declines only slightly among older cohorts of Mexican Americans. However, fewer persons of Mexican American descent reach old age. Newton and Ruiz (1981) show that Chicanos of both sexes die younger than others because, as a rule, they lead lives of poverty, and suffer the effects of strenuous physical labor. Additionally, Mexican-American women are taxed by giving birth to and raising large numbers of children.

The majority of older Hispanics are foreign born. Valle and Mendoza (1978), for example, found that 64 percent of the Mexican Americans they studied in and around San Diego were foreign born, and all of the older Puerto Ricans they contacted had come from the Island of Puerto Rico. A survey in Los Angeles showed that 34 percent of elderly Mexican Americans were foreign born (Castillo, 1978). Yet, in Sotomayor's 1973 study of older Mexican-American grandparents in Denver, only 8 percent identified themselves as foreign born. These data suggest that the proportion of foreign born Mexican Americans may decrease as the population becomes more distant from the Mexican-American border. Although no statistics on the nativity of Cuban Americans were located, it is assumed that most elderly Cubans are foreign born since the vast majority of them came to the mainland U.S. during the past 20 to 30 years.

Education:

With regard to education, the Hispanic elderly have the second highest illiteracy rate of any ethnic group in the United States. Only older Native Americans are less educated (Velez, Verdugo and Nunez, 1981). In 1978, only nine percent of non-Hispanics age 65+ had not completed at least five years of schooling, while the corresponding figure for Hispanics was 45 percent. Although in future cohorts of Hispanic elderly this proportion will probably decrease, the educational gap between Hispanics and non-Hispanics is likely to increase as proportionally more non-Hispanics receive increasingly higher levels of education. Among Hispanics aged 45 to 64, 25 percent have had less than 5 years of schooling, compared with only three percent of the same age group of non-Hispanics; thus, Hispanics in this group are eight times more likely than non-Hispanics to be educationally deprived (U.S. Census, 1978).

Within the Hispanic population, older Cubans had a significantly higher level of education than did older Puerto Ricans or Mexican Americans. Although 21 percent of all Cubans 65 years of age or older had completed less than five years of schooling, 35 percent had completed high school or more. The latter figure compares favorably with the 39 percent of non-Hispanics 65+ years old who have completed high school. The high level of education of the current cohort of older Cubans probably reflects the over-representation of people of higher socioeconomic classes among the earliest Cuban emigres. Current census data indicate that the educational gap between Cubans and non-Hispanics will widen considerably as later, less-educated immigrants reach senior status.

In her study of New York City's inner-city elderly, Cantor (1976) found Puerto Rican immigrants had the least amount of formal education of any racial or ethnic group studied. Census data reveals that one in four Puerto Ricans, ages 45 to 64, completed less than five years of schooling, and that just over one in four completed high school or had more advanced schooling.

3

Older Mexican Americans have had considerably less formal education than other segments of the Hispanic population. Leonard (1967) reports that the Mexican-American elderly in the Southwest, three-fourths of whom are functionally illiterate, have the highest illiteracy rate in the nation for older persons. Carp's (1969) study of older low-income Mexican Americans living in San Antonio revealed that nearly half had no formal schooling. The majority were illiterate in both English and Spanish, and less than 10 percent could read or speak English.

In San Diego, among Valle and Mendoza's (1978) sample of elderly Hispanics (88% of whom were Mexican American), 23 percent had no formal education, and the average number of years of schooling was 5.8. Similarly, Torres-Gil and Becerra (1977) found that 25 percent of the Mexican American elderly they studied in San Jose, California had no formal education. Finally, the University of Southern California Community Survey of Los Angeles (1977) showed that 70 percent of older Mexican-American males and 86 percent of the females (age 65-74) had six or fewer years of education.

It is difficult to assess the socio-psychological effects of educational deprivation on older Hispanics. Formal education is a resource typically acquired in youth. The effects of this deprivation on Hispanic adults who continue to learn informally from the experience of living is unknown.

Income:

The results of low educational achievement among Hispanics is reflected in smaller financial rewards for their occupational performance. According to the Bureau of the Census (1980), in 1979 the median income for Hispanic families in the United States was $14,711. This was significantly less than the $20,840 median income for non-Hispanic families. Median incomes also varied substantially by national origin: from a high of $16,200 per year for Cuban families to a low of $10,000 annually for Puerto Rican families. Mexican-American families fell between these two extremes with an annual income of $15,200. Twenty-four percent of all Hispanic families fell below the poverty level, compared with 9 percent of non-Hispanic families. Since Hispanic families generally are larger than other families, having a mean number of 3.9 persons compared with 3.3 persons in non-Hispanic families, their smaller incomes have to stretch considerably further to support larger families (U.S. Bureau of the Census, 1980).

Occupation:

By comparing statistics on the occupational status of Anglos and Hispanics, a major reason for the ethnic discrepancy in income becomes clear. Hispanics are significantly less likely than members of the total labor force to be employed in higher-paying occupations. Hispanic are more likely than non-Hispanic males to work in blue-collar occupations (58% vs. 45%), and only half as likely as non-Hispanics to be employed in white-collar occupations (24% vs. 43%). Due to the over-representation of women in clerical and associated white-collar occupations, the proportion of both Hispanic and non-Hispanic females in this category exceeds that of their male counterparts. Nevertheless while about one in every two Hispanic females who works is classified as a white-collar worker, about two out of every three non-Hispanic females are similarly categorized. Moreover, Hispanic women are twice as likely as their non-Hispanic peers to hold blue-collar positions (28% vs. 14%).

According to census data, Hispanics are most likely to be employed as operatives--laundry workers, garage workers, or service workers--all blue-collar classifications. This contrasts with statistics on the total civilian labor force where clerical work and professional-technical work, both white-collar classifications, have the highest proportion of workers. Hispanics are about half as likely as workers in general to have professional or technical jobs (8% vs 15%), and are about three times more likely to work as farm laborers (3% vs. 1%) (U.S. Census, 1978).

Within the Hispanic working population, the most conspicuous differences in occupational status exist between males of Cuban origin and Mexican Americans and Puerto Ricans. Compared to men in the other two Hispanic groups, Cuban males are occupationally advantaged. They are more than two times as likely as Puerto Ricans, and more than three times as likely as Mexican Americans, to hold professional or technical positions. In fact, Cuban males are slightly more likely to hold this type of occupation than are males in the general labor force (17% vs. 15%). Cuban males also occupy managerial and administrative positions in the same proportion as males in the general labor force (14%), which makes them more than twice as likely to be employed in this category as Mexican-American or Puerto Rican males (5% and 7%, respectively).

On the lower end of the occupational spectrum, seven percent of Mexican-American males are employed as farm laborers and supervisors, while only two percent of Puerto Rican males, and a statistically insignificant number of Cuban males (U.S. Census, 1978) are similarly employed. Because of problems involved in counting seasonal migrant workers and undocumented residents, these numbers are probably very conservative.

Measures of occupational status alone, however, do not fully explain the contrast in income levels between Hispanics and non-Hispanics. With the exception of farm laborers and service workers, Hispanics consistently earn less on the average than their non-Hispanic counterparts working in the same occupational category. As Moore (1970) points out, this reflects the fact that Hispanics hold the lower-level jobs within each occupational category.

5

These demographics point out that Hispanics in general, and the Hispanic elderly specifically, suffer shorter life spans, are poorly educated, have fewer financial rewards, and tend to occupy positions in the lowest rungs of the occupational ladder.

B. IMMIGRATION AND GEOGRAPHICAL DISTRIBUTION

The particular reasons why and the conditions under which members of Hispanic populations emigrated has a significant effect on their experiences in the U.S., and largely determines their attitudes and the cultural context of their life. For these reasons, an understanding of the disparate economic, geographical, historical and social conditions that brought Cubans, Mexican Americans, and Puerto Ricans to the U.S. may provide insight into the life experience of elderly Hispanic Americans of each national origin.

Puerto Ricans

All residents of the Island of Puerto Rico are U.S. citizens; therefore, it is technically inaccurate to speak of immigration when referring to Puerto Ricans who come to the mainland U.S. to live. These persons can move freely from la isla to the continental U.S. and back as often as they choose. For this reason, the actual data on the exact numbers of elderly Puerto Ricans may be higher than recorded in the Census because it is believed that older Puerto Ricans return to Puerto Rico to retire or spend a significant amount of time on the Island.

To whatever extent this outmigration has occurred in the past, Cantor (1976) believes the phenomenon is fading with each succeeding generation of Puerto Ricans. De Armas (1975), however, believes that the low census count of older Puerto Rican residents is due to the inability of enumerators to locate them, and the shorter longevity of this group compared with that of the general U.S. population.

The largest wave of Puerto Ricans came to the mainland during the postwar industrial boom of the 1950's. Their own economy was stagnant, and employment opportunities in the Northeast U.S. were good. New arrivals settled predominantly in East Harlem, where today 50 percent of the population is of Puerto Rican heritage. Other large Puerto Rican communities formed in Chicago, Philadelphia, and in the Tri-State area surrounding New York City (Donaldson and Martinez, 1980).

Because Puerto Ricans settled in industrial centers of the East more often than other Hispanics, they tend to live in inner-cities. Four out of five live in central cities, while less than one in 20 resides in a nonmetropolitan area (U.S. Census, 1978). This situation has both positive and negative effects on elderly Puerto Rican residents of the U.S. While it means older migrants probably live within close proximity to an ethnic community in which traditional goods and services and an informal social-support system are available, it also means they are more likely to be targets for criminals, have more health problems, and that they are more likely to face other problems that result from living in urban centers (Cantor, 1976).

Cuban Americans

Cuban Americans, like Puerto Ricans, are relative newcomers to the mainland U.S. Mass emigration from Cuba began during the Cuban revolution of 1959. The first large-scale migration, from 1959 to 1962, brought principally middle and upper-class Cubans seeking political asylum. Despite their limited economic resources, many have quickly moved up the economic ladder because they possessed professional or entrepreneural skills and talents.

Between 1962 and 1965, political circumstances all but halted Cuban migration. Then, between 1966 and 1972, a second wave of immigration brought a greater proportion of skilled, semi-skilled, and unskilled workers. In 1973, with the Cuban Government's suspension of the "freedom flight" program, which had provided a means of egress for over a quarter of a million refugees, large-scale emigration was again halted. However, restrictions were temporarily relaxed by the Cuban Government in April, 1980, leading to a new wave of immigration. Within three months it was estimated that 110,000 Cuban emigres, less than half those reputed to have filed for exit visas arrived in the U.S.

The majority of Cuban immigrants have remained in the Miami-Dade County area of Florida. Current estimates place Dade County's Cuban population at 500,000, which is one-third of the County's total population (Szapocznik and Kurtines, 1980). While there is another smaller concentration of Cubans living in Northern New Jersey, most attempts to encourage Cubans to relocate outside of Florida have been relatively unsuccessful. Even immigrants who initially settle in Northern areas tend to move back to Miami because they prefer Florida's mild climate and social conditions. It is also estimated that a majority of recent immigrants (from 50% to 75%) have remained in the greater Miami area. Consequently, almost all Hispanics of Cuban origin (97%) live in urban areas, and 37 percent of these live in the inner city. The latter group is most likely to comprise recent immigrants of lower socioeconomic status who move into high-density Hispanic areas in Dade County, Florida, such as Hialeah and "little Havana". Earlier Cuban immigrants have tended to gain affluence and move out to less dense areas of the County (Szapocznik and Kurtines, 1980).

The most recent immigrants (since 1978) have been of lower socioeconomic background and possessed fewer marketable skills than

7

their predecessors. These newer immigrants will probably change the sociodemographic profile of the Cuban American to more closely reflect that of both the Mexican American and the Puerto Rican.

Mexican Americans

Many Mexican Americans can trace their heritage back to an era before the U.S. Southwest was part of the United States. Most Mexican Americans, however, trace their Mexican heritages back to more recent immigration waves. Immigration from Mexico has continued through many generations, thus, the elderly Mexican-American population includes both foreign-born and native-born Americans.

Whether they crossed the border legally or illegally, most migrants from Mexico ended up at the bottom of the economic ladder. As agricultural workers, they labored strenuously for long hours for very low pay, lived in extremely poor housing, suffered from little or no health care, and had little or no contact with the outside Anglo world. Memories of these circumstances predominate in the minds of many of today's elderly Mexican Americans, as do rememberances of mass deportation programs instituted by local and Federal officials in the U.S. during the 1930's. These deportation programs were conceived and instituted because the public mistakenly believed that migrant laborers from Mexico were becoming permanent recipients of charitable funds (Moore, 1970).

The growing number of undocumented residents of Mexican descent became a serious concern during the Depression when Mexican laborers living in the U.S. were displaced from their jobs by Anglo immigrants coming West to flee the Midwestern dust bowl. The economic bases of the Southwestern cities were simply unable to supply this unemployed population with relief funds. Consequently, to reduce caseloads, the Government instituted the first program of involuntary repatriations of Mexicans to Mexico. Deportation was often carried out in violation of existing immigration statutes and, occasionally, without regard to the deportee's citizenship status. Between 1930 and 1934, 64,000 U.S. residents of Mexican origin were deported without formal proceedings (Moore, 1970).

The immigration of Mexicans to the United States peaked during the postwar periods following the First and Second World Wars when economic booms increased the demand for cheap agricultural labors. Coinciding with the institution of the "bracero" contract labor program during the period 1954 to 1964, Mexicans crossed the border with work permits which allowed them to legally work in the United States.

Then beginning in the Mid-1960's, labor unions, Northern industries, and other special interest groups began to object to laws allowing cheap labor. As industries which benefited from the availability of cheap labor (agriculture, mining, railroads, and so forth) lost political power,

8

legal avenues of entry were reduced. This led to increases in illegal immigration (Moore, 1970). The result was what has come to be known unofficially as "Operation Wetback", which accounted for the deportation of approximately 3.8 million Mexicans. With the passage of the Immigration Reform Act of 1965, the U.S.-Mexican border was "closed". Immigration to the U.S. from Mexico has been limited since then to 20,000 persons annually.

Strict immigration laws and mass deportation, however, have not halted the migration of Mexicans into the United States. Historically, several factors have encouraged movements across the border to the U.S.: first, the dissolution of the peonage system as a result of the Mexican Revolution of 1910 enabled poor Mexican farm laborers to leave their peonage to seek work on farms in the Southwestern U.S.; second, the completion of railroad connections to the Mexican interior provided a means of transportation for Mexican workers; third, the introduction of capital and labor-intensive irrigation farming to the Southwest created a demand for seasonal wage labor.

According to Grebler et. al. (1970), migration has taken the form of a back-and-forth movement across the border because the need for cheap labor in the U.S. ebbs and flows, and there is a fluctuation in the degree of immigration control exercised by the U.S. Government. This is consistent with the findings of most researchers who state that migrant laborers come to the U.S. only temporarily to work the harvests and then return to their families in Mexico until they again cross the border to earn money during the next picking season.

The majority of the current generation of older Mexican Americans has had to adopt to two major relocations: the move from Mexico to the U.S., and the shift from a rural to an urban setting. Sanchez (1974) identifies urbanization as the more disruptive of these two migrations. The movement from rural Mexico to the rural Southwest early in this century (1900-1930) represented only a modest cultural shock for Mexican emigrants because in the rural U.S. they tended to work and live in ethnically homogeneous rural settings. These rural communities were minimally influenced by Anglo-American culture, and retained many customs of traditional Mexican culture. They provided support for traditional family structures which emphasized the elderly male's role as an authority in agricultural skills (Sanchez, 1974) and the elderly female's importance in childrearing. This rural heritage, shared by the majority of foreign-born and native-born Mexican Americans, came to an end, however, with the increasing mechanization of agriculture, with the "bracero" program of seasonal labor, and with the movement of rural populations to urban areas.

Yet, even as late as 1950, one-third (32%) of the Hispanics living in the Southwest resided in non-urban areas (Leonard, 1967). By 1978 only 19 percent of the Mexican American population resided in nonmetropolitan areas (U.S. Census, 1978). Almost half (46%) of the remaining 81 percent lived in inner cities, including a majority of all elderly Mexican Americans.

The extent to which discrimination contributed to deportations is difficult to assess. Although the government policies may have been based on economic considerations, the result of programs such as "Operation Wetback" was that almost all U.S. residents of Mexican descent perceived these actions as proof that they were not welcome in the U.S. Today this feeling still prevails, especially among older U.S. residents of Mexican-American descent.

C. THE FAMILY

In no other area of Hispanic gerontology is research as contradictory as that on the role of older persons in the family. Additionally, virtually all such research has focused on the Mexican-American elderly residing in the Southwest. Because the lifestyles of Hispanics of disparate cultural heritages differ considerably from the lifestyles of residents of different regions in the U.S., these data only suggest possible patterns.

Most early work on Mexican-American families has focused on those cultural folk traditions that differentiate family-life in Mexico from that in the U.S. Because the more isolated, rural Mexican residents of the Southwest, who are least acculturated into the American lifestyle, are most likely to exhibit these traditional family patterns, they have been chosen most often as subjects for research on Hispanic family life (Bell, et al., 1976). Only in the last few years have family researchers become interested in more acculturated urban dwellers.

The most widely used methodological approach to understanding Mexican families has been the ethnographic method which, while an excellent method in one sense, has tended to romanticize the social roles of older family members in traditional Mexican-American families. By so doing it inhibits an understanding of the problems and hardships these elderly persons actually face. Additionally, highlighting cultural differences between Hispanic and Anglo families prompts Anglos to view Hispanic families as not only different from their own, but as dysfunctional in terms of satisfactory adjustment to life in the U.S. Most importantly, data describing family-life in relatively non-acculturated segments of the Mexican-American population often are used to generalize about all Mexican Americans (Bell, et al., 1976; Laurel, 1976).

Many critics of this research do not dispute early descriptions of the make-up and values of traditional Mexican-American families and how these structures and roles differ from Anglo family relationships; however, they do disagree with the view that the typically tight-knit, extended family structure characteristic of traditional Hispanic families act as a barrier to acculturation. In fact, they suggest the strong social ties in such families may act as social support systems benefiting the psychological health of family members, particularly among families where pressures of living as a minority are greatest. Moreover, they seriously doubt that descriptions of traditional Mexican family structures accurately depict the lifestyles and circumstances of the majority of Mexican Americans living in the U.S. today.

Traditional Structure

The traditional structure of the Mexican family grew out of the socio-economic needs dictated by the agrarian and craft economies of Mexico. For the traditional Mexican, the word family meant an extended, multigenerational group of persons, with specific social roles ascribed to members of each age group. By dividing functions and responsibilities among differing generations of family members, the family was able to perform all the economic and social support chores necessary for survival in the relatively Spartan environment of rural Mexico. Mutual support, sustenance, and interaction between family members during both work and leisure hours, dominates lives of persons in these traditional Mexican families (Miranda, 1975).

Elderly members of traditional, extended families were presumably spared many of the hazards to physical and psychological well-being usually associated with disengagement from active working roles. For men and women too old to work, adult children provided economic support and assistance with housekeeping. At the same time, because grandparents were given specific social roles to perform, older persons continued to be valued members of the family. Their expertise and importance as role models gave them status and authority highly respected by younger family members (Maldonado, 1975).

There is evidence that Hispanics in the U.S., more than other persons, believe in this extended family orientation. Analyses of data concerning elderly residents of Los Angeles show that while Black and white respondents generally conform to dominant Anglo-American family patterns (i.e., dominance of the nuclear family), Mexican Americans live differently and have different expectations and opinions about familism (i.e., stronger commitment to extended family relationships) (Bengtson and Burton, 1980). The variation in these indicators of familism cannot be accounted for by differences in socioeconomic status or sex of respondents (Manuel and Bengtson, 1976). Sotomayor's (1973) study of Mexican-American grandparents suggests that essentially traditional attitudes about intergenerational family roles and relationships are held by older Hispanics living in Denver. Valle and Mendoza (1978), however, found that elderly Latinos in San Diego were less traditional in their family attitudes, but continued to rely on the support of family members in times of need.

11

In Cantor's (1976) study in New York City, Puerto Rican elders also were members of extended families in which frequent interaction and direct mutual assistance was commonplace. Likewise, Cuban families have been characterized as having strong intergenerational ties in that older persons often live with adult children and their families, or are supported by them in other ways which prevent the need for institutionalization in older age (U.S. Senate, Special Committee on Aging, 1971).

While these findings seem to support the idea that the extended family supportive of its elderly continues to operate in the U.S., a second group of investigations contradicts this. Nunez, (1975) and Maldonado (1975) believe rapid social change is breaking down the traditional extended family and that as a consequence, older Chicanos, as well as Anglos, are suffering from isolation and alienation. According to Maldonado (1975), as younger generations of Hispanics rise in social status, they become more mobile and increase the physical distance between themselves and their kin thereby decreasing familial interdependence. Urbanization, modernization, and increased acculturation among young Mexican Americans also has tended to strengthen nuclear family ties and weaken links to extended family members. Hence, Mexican-American elders may suddenly find themselves relatively alone in an "alien" culture without the type of support they value and expect.

Solis's (1975) research supports the contention that extended-family structures and social support systems among Hispanics are eroding, so that today a significant number of elderly Hispanics are isolated both residentially and socially, and are subject to possible institutionalization. Positive alternatives to aging within the extended family context may be inaccessible to older Chicanos. The situation is particularly acute because while Anglo elderly have been defining social roles and lifestyles compatible with growing older without family support, Miranda (1975) reports that most older Hispanics have insufficient economic resources to pursue these new, independent lifestyles.

But the facts support neither those who contend that traditional living patterns are a thing of the past, nor those who say extended, supportive family structures still exist for a majority of U.S. Hispanics. For on the one hand, while there is no doubt that urbanization and modernization are making the traditional paradigm untenable for many older Hispanics today, a great deal of evidence indicates that rather than disappearing, the extended family structure is being modified to fit changing economic, social, and cultural conditions.

The Extended Family

Hispanic families in the United States are, on the average, larger

12

than non-Spanish families. While the average non-Hispanic family in 1978 included 3.3 persons, the average Mexican-American family contained 4.1 persons, Puerto Rican families contained 3.8 persons, and Cuban families contained 3.5 persons. Recent national fertility statistics, however, suggest Hispanic nuclear families may be getting smaller (U.S. Census, 1978).

The fact that Hispanics tend to have larger families than non-Hispanics is seen in the increased number of living children and grandchildren of older Mexican Americans. In 1976, only 5 percent of Mexican Americans age 60 and over in Los Angeles had no surviving children, in contrast to 20 percent of whites. Additionally, 34 percent of Mexican Americans, ages 60+, also were more likely to have at least one grandchild: 92 percent, as opposed to 82 percent of white respondents and 70 percent of Black respondents (Bengtson and Burton, 1980). Among Sotomayor's (1973) sample of urban Chicano grandparents, the median number of living adult children was four, and the median number of grandchildren was twelve. Large numbers of children and grandchildren are important in extended family structures because they provide a basis of social support for older adults.

Unlike Anglo-American nuclear-family structures, traditional Mexican extended-families include non-blood-related persons, or fictive kin. This fictive kinship bond, usually between parent and godparents, is one of the most important relationships within the traditional Mexican family. It serves as a prototype for all significant peer relationships (Moore, 1970). While empirical data concerning the present state of this fictive kinship system or "compadrazgo" among Mexican Americans is admittedly limited, it suggests the institution no longer plays as important a role as it originally did. Sotomayor (1973) found, for instance, that 40 percent of the "compadres" of elderly Mexican-American grandparents in Denver were actually blood kin and were the "compadres" with whom respondents most frequently interacted. Similarly, Keefe et al. (1979) found that among a sample of Southern California Mexican Americans, only blood kin "compadres" were likely to be included in familial support networks. These results indicate that the current form of the Mexican American extended family no longer includes fictive kin.

The Family as a Special Support

While elderly Hispanics have relatively many more living descendants than in the past, this does not necessarily mean they grow old within an extended family network. Maldonado (1975) notes that the numbers of relatives an older person has is not as important as the extent of communication and interaction between that person and his or her kin. Data show that elderly Mexican Americans interact more frequently with family members, and are more satisfied with the frequency of that family interaction than are whites or Blacks (Bengtson and Burton,

1980). Elderly Mexican Americans not only interacted more frequently with kin than did members of other ethnic groups, but also attributed their satisfaction with these relationships to this more frequent interaction. This suggests that elderly Chicanos had greater interactional expectations than Anglos, which lends support to Keefe et al.'s (1979) hypothesis that the potential for deleterious effects upon morale caused by unmet interactional expectations are more serious among Chicano elderly than among older Anglos or Blacks (Nunez, 1975).

Dowd and Bengtson (1978) state that while Anglo elderly tend to increase interaction with friends and neighbors during post-retirement years, older Chicanos continue to exhibit the same low levels of interaction with friends and neighbors that characterized their pre-retirement years. This indicates that primary social interaction, in the past and in the present for older Mexican Americans, takes place within the family.

Keefe et al. (1979) learned that Mexican Americans are more likely than Anglos to have large numbers of relatives living close by (see also Sotomayor, 1973; Valle and Mendoza, 1978). The primary difference between Anglo and Chicano support networks was that Anglos were more likely than Chicanos to seek support from neighbors and friends while Mexican Americans were more likely than Anglos to seek help exclusively from other family members. These Hispanic family support systems were well integrated, intergenerational, and limited to blood kin: fictive kin ("compadres") were rarely called on to provide emotional support.

Historically the extended family took responsibility for the welfare and financial support of older Mexican-American family members no longer able to work. And typically, in rural areas, the primary burden fell upon older adult sons (Leonard, 1967). However, as the economy shifted from agrarian to industrial, the functions of elderly support have been transferred to governmental institutions (Miranda, 1975). The degree to which elderly urban Hispanics have become acculturated to this Anglo-American norm of state support for the elderly has been the subject of debate among gerontologists for over a decade. Carp (1968) reports that urban Mexican Americans still prefer to care for their own elderly, and that failure to do so is seen as deviant behavior in Mexican-American communities. Consequently, few elderly Chicanos are found among institutionalized populations of older persons (Newton and Ruiz, 1979).

Other authors are less convinced that the extended family in its urban form follows the tradition of assuming responsibility for the welfare of its elderly members. Penalosa (1967) reports that 61 percent of Mexican-American adults in Southern California said the family did not have an obligation to support the elderly. A number of scholars attribute this change to the effects of acculturation, urbanization, and contemporary economics. Laurel (1976) showed in a Texas study

14

that filial responsibility was negatively associated with youth, urban residence, higher socioeconomic status, and greater generational distance from immigrant ancestry. Neither sex nor religious affiliation of respondents was significantly associated with perceptions of filial responsibility. Rural residency was the variable most strongly associated with greater willingness to assume responsibility for the care of elderly parents. Laurel (1976) suggests this is true because stronger social pressures to conform to traditional filial patterns exist in rural areas, whereas Crouch (1972) attributes rural-urban differences to the deprived economic circumstances of most Hispanics living in urban areas.

Maldonado (1975) reports that elderly Mexican Americans are becoming more independent because they recognize it would be economically difficult for their adult children to support them. Yet 95 percent of the older Chicanos in Sotomayor's (1973) Denver study indicated that, if they could no longer care for themselves, they would expect relatives to take care of them, either in their own home or in the relative's home. Moreover, Bengtson and Burton (1980) found that 66 percent of older Mexican Americans agreed it was the obligation of adult children to care for older parents. However, only one-third expected to move in with their adult children if they no longer could live alone. Whites were only about half as likely to evince these expectations of filial support. In contrast to these findings, two-thirds of elderly Hispanics in Crouch's study (1972) felt the family was not obligated to care for older members. Clearly, traditional attitudes about filial responsibility for the care of older persons still exist in part in certain groups, but here, too, this tradition is being eroded.

Grandparenting

What is the role of elderly in the Hispanic family? Among rural Mexican-American families, Leonard (1967) says grandparents have three primary roles: as religious advocates and teachers, as childrearers, and as participants in family decision-making. Both Leonard (1967) and Sotomayor (1975) believe that the role of elderly extended family members in decision-making belies popular mythology supporting the idea that all family authority rests in the hands of Hispanic men in traditional extended families.

While there are few studies on the topic, existing findings suggest elderly Hispanics do continue to play important roles in family decision-making in urban extended families. Cantor (1976) found older Puerto Ricans were twice as likely as elderly Blacks or whites to exert influence in family decision-making, childrearing, and in advising others. Sotomayor (1973) learned that 94 percent of the urban Chicano grandparents felt grandmothers were influential in family life, while 87 percent perceived grandfathers to be influential. Nearly identical proportions of respondents felt that the opinions of grandfathers and grandmothers were respected, and that their influential roles were

15

due to their long life experience and value as role models, rather than solely due to the respect and love of younger family members. About four-fifths of these older Hispanics said they were satisfied with their perceived influence on their families (Sotomayor, 1973).

The family importance attributed to grandmothers among Sotomayor's urban respondents also is shown in Leonard's (1967) research on rural Hispanic extended families. He found that the woman's role in decision-making and advising increases as she grows older. This further deflates the popular conception of the Mexican-American family as exclusively patriarchal.

Childrearing was perceived by Sotomayor's (1973) respondents as one of the principal functions of grandparents living within the family, and older persons were more likely to consider their roles with grandchildren as instructional (53%) or caretaking (37%), rather than as affective (87%). Grandparents of both sexes see themselves as being about equally responsible for childrearing, and considered their most important tasks to be teaching grandchildren to speak Spanish and to learn traditional customs, morality, and religious behavior. In addition, one in four older persons stressed the importance of encouraging formal education among grandchildren.

While belief in the importance of grandparents' instilling traditional customs and values among grandchildren was strong among Sotomayor's (1973) older respondents, few persons mentioned other traditional aspects of grandparenting such as the role of the Mexican grandfather as family historian, or the grandmother's duty to pass on information concerning the preparation of native foods or use of medicinal herbs. In addition, while 86 percent of these older urban residents felt grandmothers had the responsibility to teach and practice religion, only 26 percent of the sample attended church regularly. This represents a change from Leonard's (1967) description of religious life among rural Mexican-American elderly who characteristically attended church several times per week. Intergenerational conflict, in the form of growing resistance of the young to learn and speak Spanish, also contributed to the further erosion of traditional functions of Mexican-American grandparents (Sotomayor, 1973).

D. THE LIVING ENVIRONMENT

Living Arrangements

Findings of numerous surveys indicate older Mexican Americans are far more likely to live in households with relatives than are elderly non-Hispanics (Torres-Gil, et. al., 1977; Valle and Mendoza, 1978; Sotomayor, 1973). Survey findings also suggest traditional intergenerational family bonds are still present. Cantor (1976) found

16

that elderly Puerto Rican respondents were more likely than either their Black or white counterparts to be living in the same home with a child.

Leonard (1967) states that among rural Mexican Americans, when adult children do not live with their elderly parents, grandchildren often are sent as companions to live with grandparents. Sotomayor (1973), in contrast, found that in most situations where elderly urban Mexican Americans live with their grandchildren, the arrangement was precipitated by a family crisis. When asked why they were raising grandchildren, 44 percent of these grandparents cited the child's coming from a broken home (i.e., illegitimacy, alcoholism, drug abuse, prison, separation or divorce), while 36 percent cited specific economic problems related to the grandchild's parent. Only 20 percent of the grandparents gave companionship as the reasons why they were raising a grandchild. These findings suggest that the practice of grandparents raising grandchildren in urban areas represents a form of direct aid to parents rather than the provision of companionship or support for grandparents. Because information on this subject is limited, it must be assumed that even where traditional patterns of intergenerational contact are found, the reasons for them may differ significantly according to the geographical area or cultural group being surveyed.

While Mexican-American elderly frequently reside in households in which grandchildren or adult children are present, this does not necessarily mean they are economically or emotionally dependent members of those households. In fact, Sotomayor (1973) learned that in all but two of the 30 extended family households she studied, adult children, grandchildren, and other relations lived in the elderly respondents' house. Carp (1969) also found Mexican-American grandparents were more likely than whites to live in intergenerational settings, and more often considered themselves or their spouses to be the head of the family. Laurel (1976) indicates that elderly Mexican Americans are more concerned than whites about loss of autonomy or head-of-household status when they must move into their adult children's homes than they are with financial ramifications of such a move.

The belief that Mexican-American elderly place a high value upon their independence from adult children is further corroborated by data on attitudes toward independent living arrangements. While older Mexican Americans were more amenable to the idea of living with children than either older Black or older white respondents, most Mexican Americans in the USC Community Survey (1977) also agreed that older people should not live with their family. This preference for independent living arrangements is also reflected in data on actual living arrangements. More than nine out of ten (95%) of Sotomayor's (1973) sample of elderly Mexican Americans in Denver, and 91 percent of Valle and Mendoza's (1978) San Diego sample of elderly Hispanics, maintained their own residences. Other family members also lived

17

in many of these households. Among those older Hispanics in San Diego who did not live independently in their own homes, only half were satisfied with their living arrangements. Similarly, Cantor (1976) found that 82 percent of elderly Puerto Ricans in her New York survey lived independently. Although this proportion was lower than that among whites, Cantor points out that given the extended family tradition and pressures of poverty, more Puerto Ricans lived independently than might have been expected.

The apparent desire for independent living arrangements among Hispanic elderly would appear to contradict the assumption that older Hispanics continue to move into their adult children's households as members of extended families. Martinez (1979) and Maldonado (1975) point out, however, that intergenerational relationships embodied by extended-family networks are not necessarily reflected in residency patterns but in proximity to kin. This preference for living independently while retaining intergenerational relationships, characteristic of the rural extended-family system, appears to be one of the major modifications of family life made by urban Hispanics. At the same time this desire to live independently may also come from the traditional desire of the older Hispanic to maintain the role of head of household within the extended family.

Housing

Elderly Hispanics are a relatively stable residential population. Sotomayor (1973) reports that median length of residency among older Hispanics in Denver is eight years, while 75 percent have lived in their current home for at least four years. In San Diego over half of the elderly Hispanic respondents had lived at their current address for at least six years. Less than one in ten said they had moved to a new location within the past year (Valle and Mendoza, 1978).

Although the Mexican-American elderly tend to be extremely disadvantaged financially, a substantial number own their own homes (Estrada, 1976). In San Antonio three out of five (60%) older Mexican Americans owned residences (Carp, 1969), while two out of three (67%) of the Mexican Americans in Los Angeles owned their own homes (Torres-Gil et al., 1977). In San Diego almost half (46%) of the Hispanics owned homes (Valle and Mendoza, 1978) and one out of four (24%) owned residences in Denver (Sotomayor, 1973). Because most elderly Hispanics reside in homes built before 1950, (Estrada, 1976) one might assume they bought these homes many years ago, and are therefore likely to have paid off their mortgages. This was in fact the case for two-thirds of the Hispanic homeowners in San Diego (Valle and Mendoza, 1978); however, rental and ownership patterns differ geographically. In San Diego (Valle and Mendoza, 1978) and Denver (Sotomayor, 1973), approximately 50 percent of Hispanics rent homes, whereas in Los Angeles only one in three rent rather than own (Torres-Gil, et al., 1977). Both

18

Sotomayor (1973) and Torres-Gil et al. (1977) find that elderly Hispanic renters are more likely to rent single-family dwellings than apartments.

Compared with older whites, elderly Hispanics live in poor quality housing. According to the 1970 Census, two to three times more Hispanics than whites live in houses that lack either toilet or bathtub, piped hot or cold water; or they share toilet or bathing facilities with another resident. Persons in the oldest cohort (65+) of Hispanics are most likely to live in such substandard housing (Bell, et al., 1976). Most homes of older Mexican Americans in the rural Southwest lack running water, flush toilets, and refrigerators. Plumbing and refrigerators, when in existence, are frequently in dilapidated condition (Leonard, 1967). Carp (1969) learned that when she compared the matched samples of poor elderly Hispanics and Anglos in San Antonio, the Hispanics' residences were generally less adequate. Similarly, 44 percent of Los Angeles's Mexican Americans compared with only 16 percent of their white counterparts said the disrepair of their homes was a serious problem (Torres-Gil, et al., 1977).

Regional variations in living environments have been noted by Bell et. al., (1976), who characterized housing as "best in the West and worst in the South." Older Mexican Americans in the central U.S. were about three times more likely to live in substandard housing than Westerners, and older Hispanics in Southern states were about five times more likely to live in poor housing than their western counterparts.

Despite the comparative inadequacy of their housing, Carp (1969) found that for older Mexican Americans, physical characteristics of a home seem to be less important to satisfaction with living circumstances than the network of supportive relationships the person has built up among neighbors and nearby kin (Carp, 1969). While Bell et al., (1976) and Moore (1971) question this conclusion, other surveys appear to support Carp's contention (Valle and Mendoza, 1978; Torres-Gil, et al., 1977).

The type of housing available to the majority of poor persons, however, may be less appropriate to the lifestyle of older Hispanics than to that of older Anglos. Because low-income elderly Hispanics tend to live with their children, grandchildren or other kin more often than older whites, the lack of housing units large enough to accomodate extended family living arrangements constitutes an added housing problem for older Cubans, Puerto Ricans, and Mexican Americans. According to testimony given before the U.S. Senate Special Committee on Aging (1971), the Cuban tradition of living in extended families may provide important social support to Cuban elderly, but it often means living in overcrowded conditions because of the small size of housing generally available in low-income urban centers. Because of limited space in crowded dwellings in the inner cities of the Northeast, older Puerto Ricans must often move and find their own quarters. Similarly, Cantor (1976) suggests it will not be long before elderly Puerto Ricans will

19

be unable to live with their adult children because no apartments suitable for large families will be available. Addressing the needs of older Mexican Americans, both Martinez (1979) and Torres-Gil, et al., (1977) suggest that alternative forms of public housing are needed to satisfy the requirements of extended families so that elderly Hispanics can continue to receive the support and sustenance of living with kin.

The Neighborhood

Many elderly Mexican Americans began their lives in the U.S. in a rural environment, and for a variety of reasons entered the modern industrialized world of the inner cities. Whether because of preference to living in proximity to other Hispanics or because of low-income housing needs, they moved to areas of high Hispanic concentrations.

Despite the poor physical environment often found in these ethnic enclaves or barrios, studies of life satisfaction among older Mexican Americans living in urban areas indicate a relatively high proportion are satisfied with their lives in these communities (Sotomayor, 1973; Valle and Mendoza, 1978; Castillo, 1978). Satisfaction among older persons with living in the barrio probably result from the supportive cultural and social context the neighborhood provides them. According to Korte (1978), moving from a rural to an urban environment may lead persons to adopt values, attitudes and expectations characteristic of both the traditional rural environment and of the modern urban life style. Because the barrio embodies characteristics of both cultures, it may cushion the impact of discontinuities associated with urbanization, acculturation to Anglo-American norms, and the move away from traditional forms of social interaction.

Sotomayor (1973) believes barrio residents are at least partially insulated from negative interactions with members of the hostile dominant society. Barrio residents are able to continue to communicate in their native language and to preserve their native culture and customs. Within the community, extended family ties can be maintained, providing older residents with both social status and support, and facilitating social interaction within the neighborhood.

Older Mexican Americans who wanted to remain in the barrio most often cited convenience of location, and positive feelings about the familiarity of the location, and their desire to be close to family, friends and neighbors (Torres-Gil, et al., 1977). These findings are also supported by Valle and Mendoza (1978) and Sotomayor (1973).

Both Sotomayor (1973) and Valle and Mendoza (1978) described these close interpersonal relationships as mutual helping networks. Sotomayor (1973) says these supportive social ties help residents cope with the crisis of poverty, job discrimination, and unemployment, problems caused by use of a different language and pressure to adhere to customs from the majority population. Older persons also benefit from these close social relationships because they maintain status and gain ego reinforcement by being able to help others in return (Valle and Mendoza, 1978).

The barrio, however, is not completely socially and culturally self-contained. Cultural attitudes and beliefs of the dominant society enter the barrio through the public school system and television. Both these influences contribute to the relatively rapid acculturation of younger Hispanics (Sotomayor, 1973). More significantly, barrios are not self-contained economically. Their poverty makes them, of necessity, dependent upon economic institutions of the dominant society for their welfare (Moore, 1970; Sotomayor, 1973). According to Sotomayor (1973), these economic constraints (principally, the lack of resources entering the community), not the physical segregation of Hispanics from the rest of society, contributes most to negative aspects of living in the barrio.

The tenuous economy of the barrio makes residents particularly susceptible to being displaced due to redevelopment through urban renewal, or the complete razing of residential areas to make way for freeways, or the development and expansion of private businesses and industries (Cuellar, 1978; Korte, 1981; Moore, 1970). Elderly barrio residents who tend to rely most heavily on social-support networks in the barrio have the most to lose when their neighborhoods are destroyed. Recognizing how easily members of the majority culture can make decisions that will threaten the security of their neighborhoods, elderly Hispanics may oppose any activities of barrio residents that will focus attention on their communities. Torres-Gil (1976) found, for example, that older Mexican Americans in San Jose, California disapproved of the goals and tactics of the Chicano movement because they feared it would bring the barrio to the attention of authorities.

Because abrupt environmental changes are more debilitating to elderly persons than slower changes of acculturation and modernization urban planners and policy-makers must recognize the barrio as a socially interconnected community rather than a collection of dilapidated structures waiting for the sledge hammer. Urban renewal may improve the physical structures of the barrio but, it cannot replicate the "fabric of meaning" torn down with the buildings (Korte, 1981).

E. RETIREMENT AND INCOME

Attitudes Toward Retirement

Although retirement usually refers to the withdrawal of older workers from the labor force, in a broader sense it also refers to the social role that older persons adopt as they define their new lifestyle.

Both contemporary and scholarly orientations toward aging reflect a tacit acceptance of the assumption that it is natural and beneficial to both the individual and society for the elderly to withdraw from the work force (McConnell, et al., 1979).

Moore (1971), however, questions the applicability of this middle-class Anglo paradigm of retirement to older, lower-SES Mexican Americans. Older Mexican Americans, according to Moore, do not terminate working careers abruptly by retiring. Rather, they are gradually and prematurely displaced from the labor market as employment opportunities wane, or as illness curtails their activities. The continuance of childrearing responsibilities into older age due to childbearing in the extended family reduces the social mobility of older Hispanic females. Their attitudes and experiences during retirement years, therefore, differ markedly from those of their middle-class Anglo counterparts. For these reasons, retirement as defined by Anglos may not be viewed positively by Mexican Americans and other Hispanics.

Recent cross-ethnic studies of Anglo and Mexican-American retirees tend to support Moore's hypothesis. Data collected in the USC Community Survey (1977) suggest the institution of retirement is not perceived as positively among older Mexican Americans as it is among older Anglos. When asked to enumerate the three things they like most about being their age, only one in every one hundred older Mexican-American men and women mentioned retirement. This compares with 16 in every one hundred older white females. A study of retired Mexican-American and Anglo males in Arizona and New Mexico (Dieppa, 1977), found significant differences in attitudes toward retirement. Mexican Americans tended to have less positive attitudes toward retirement and its effect on their lives. In particular, Mexican-American retired persons were more than three times as likely than retired Anglos to feel retirement was "a waste of time." More frequently than Anglos, they found themselves with nothing to do.

Perhaps the most significant indicator of the difference between retirement experiences of Anglo and Hispanic workers is reflected in a comparison of their self-reported reasons for retirement. While older Anglos typically said they retired voluntarily at around age 65, the typical response of Hispanics was that they were forced out of the labor market because of deteriorating health before they reached retirement age.

The USC Survey (1977) found that 54 percent of older white males cite health problems as a reason for retirement. In contrast, 64 percent of Mexican-American males gave poor health as a reason for their retirement. In addition, forced retirement due to advanced age was reported twice as frequently by Mexican-American males as Anglo males, and four times more frequently by Mexican-American females than Anglo women. Again, health problems seemed to explain the high incidence of retirement among Mexican-American males, 11 percent of who were retired by the age of 60 (Simonia, et al., 1978).

A comparative study in New York City of older Blacks, whites, and Puerto Ricans (Carp, 1969), showed 61 percent of Puerto Ricans aged 60-64 no longer were working, in contrast with only 25 percent of similarly aged whites. Nonworking Puerto Ricans also were two-and-one-half times more likely than nonworking whites to consider themselves retired rather than unemployed. Carp considers this to be their accurate perception that they have been irrevocably expulsed from the labor market because of poor health and minimal opportunities for employment for Puerto Ricans of this age cohort.

Early cessation of employment because of poor health has a number of dire consequences for older Hispanics. Since almost all programs designed to assist the elderly, i.e., Social Security, Medicare, and supplemental Social Security Income, require participants to be 65 years of age or older to be eligible for full benefits, workers retiring involuntarily before age 65 face retirement with little income and usually high medical expenses without recourse to a benefit program. This makes of retirement a life of poverty and poor health. That this unpleasant scenario is particularly likely to occur among elderly minorities is borne out by Dowd and Bengtson (1978). Their findings revealed that differences between white and minority responses concerning income and health are exacerbated among older age cohorts. As age increased, minority respondents showed a steeper decline in income and self-reported physical well-being than did white respondents. Dieppa (1977) also found that age-related declines in economic and physical well-being were far more prevalent among older Mexican Americans than Anglos.

An additional hypothesis about attitudes toward retirement may be that Mexican Americans have a less positive orientation to retirement because they have a more positive attachment to work than do their Anglo peers. Dieppa (1977) found that a majority of the retired male Anglo respondents answered "yes" to the question: "Is retirement easy for you to accept in your life, considering the way you were brought up?" Less than half of the retired Hispanic men, however, responded positively to the question. Anglos also were more than six times more likely than Hispanics to disagree that people should be hard working throughout their lives. Dieppa found responses to questions on work and leisure indicated that Mexican-American respondents' orientation toward work was as strong or stronger than that of Anglos. It appears that Anglos are able to change from a "work ethic" to a "leisure ethic" as they reach retirement. Hispanics, on the other hand, cling to the work ethic and therefore find it difficult to adjust to retirement.

Although current census figures contrasting occupations and incomes of Hispanics with those of non-Hispanics show Hispanics still are economically disadvantaged, the relative ethnic discrepancies in occupational status and income levels have been significantly reduced

23

in the past decade. This indicates that problems of educational disadvantage and discriminatory employment practices are gradually being rectified. Today's older Hispanics, however, who worked in times of severe occupational structures, continue to suffer these past injustices since their low-paying and low-status jobs often provide little or no old-age benefits or pensions.

In general, retirement income depends on three sources: Social Security benefits, private pension income, and savings. The lack of one or more of these sources of income tends to undermine economic security in old age because in one way or another each income source derives from a stable and relatively affluent past work-history. For example, Social Security benefits are calculated on the basis of the individual's average income during his working career. Moreover, private pension coverage is most commonly associated with higher-level occupations (McConnell, et al., 1979), and private savings are directly related to discretionary income during one's working career. As a result, 18 percent of all Hispanic families with a family head 65 years of age or older have incomes below the poverty level, as compared with 8 percent of non-Hispanics (U.S. Census, 1978).

In New York, Cantor's study (1976) of older Blacks, whites, and Puerto Ricans found that Puerto Ricans had the lowest levels of income. In Denver, Sotomayor (1973) found the majority of her sample of Mexican-American grandparents had incomes below the poverty line. In USC's Community Survey in Los Angeles (1977), retired Mexican-American males were three-and-one-half times more likely than retired white men to report annual incomes under $4000. In short, independent research projects across the United States show over and over again that elderly Hispanics, in comparison to older Anglos, face severe economic shortcomings in retirement income.

1. Social Security

Social Security, the economic base of most retirement incomes, paid benefits to approximately 91 percent of all retired persons 65 years of age or over in 1975 (McConnell, et al., 1979). Sanchez (1974) states that while 75 percent of the total population of elderly poor receive Social Security benefits, only 55 percent of elderly poor Hispanics are receiving such assistance. Cantor's (1976) cross-ethnic study of elderly persons in New York City revealed that a smaller percentage of elderly Puerto Ricans than whites or Blacks received Social Security benefits and those who did tended to receive less money. Social Security coverage among older Mexican Americans also tends to be relatively low, although the percentage of beneficiaries varies according to geography. In Los Angeles, 59 percent of retired Mexican-American males or their spouses versus 84 percent of white male retirees or their spouses had received Social Security benefits during 1976. Valle and Mendoza (1978) corroborate the findings of the Los Angeles study by showing that only

61 percent of San Diego's elderly Mexican-American population receiv
Social Security benefits. In other Southwestern states (Arizona ā
New Mexico), the percentage of Mexican-American Social Secur
beneficiaries rises to 81 percent, still below the comparable fig
of 92 percent for retired male Anglos (Dieppa, 1977). McConnell,
al., (1979) report that Hispanics tend to work in temporary or part t
jobs that are not covered under Social Security. This fact alone accoɪ
for the exclusion of at least 24 percent of elderly Mexican Americ
from Social Security because almost one in four of these minority wor
was employed irregularly or seasonally as a farm laborer.

High levels of involuntary retirement at an early age aɪ
Mexican Americans and Puerto Ricans (Cantor, 1976; McConnell
al., 1979) also account for the lower proportion of Social Sec
beneficiaries among these two groups. Although Social Security c
the option of collecting reduced benefits at age 62, the average
expectancy for Mexican Americans is only 55.6 years (McConnel
al., 1979).

Another factor which reduces the amount of Social Se
benefits Mexican Americans are likely to receive is the meth
calculating the level of Social Security support. The amoɪ
determined by computing incomeless years into an average yearly iɪ
thus, monthly payments are reduced for Hispanics who have
irregularly employed, or who have been unemployed during the nc
high earning period of late middle age (Sanchez, 1974).

2. Pensions

The Hispanic elderly are less likely to receive retirement
from private pensions than are whites. Only one in ten (11%) of
Puerto Ricans in Cantor's New York study reported that the
covered by private pensions. In contrast, one in three (33%)
whites had some income from this source. Similarly, only 9
of older Mexican-American respondents in Valle and Mendoza'
San Diego study said they were receiving income from pens
much higher percent of Mexican-American males and their
in Los Angeles were covered by pensions (38%). This was,]
considerably below the comparable figure of 61 percent for t
category of Anglos (McConnell, et. al., 1979).

Data from these studies indicate that Hispanics are underreɪ
in the population covered by private pensions. Some factors coɪ
to this dilemma include uneven employment histories; low em
in manufacturing, professional or technical jobs associated wit
plans; lack of job tenure, especially immediately before re
and low wage-earning positions.

25

3. Private Savings

Framers of the Social Security Act of 1935 assumed that income from private savings would constitute the primary source of income for retired persons. Social Security benefits were intended to supplement these savings. Today with the high cost of living and with high inflation rates reducing the real values of monies that are saved, the expectation that low-income workers can save a substantial portion of their wages in preparation for retirement is unrealistic. Hispanic retirees, a majority of whom have been low-income wage-earners, are relatively unlikely to cite personal savings as a source of income. Only 9 percent of elderly Puerto Ricans in New York City had income producing savings, in contrast with 43 percent of older whites (Cantor, 1976). Mexican-American men in Arizona and New Mexico were comparatively better off; one in three said they had savings to rely on as a source of retirement income, as opposed to one in two Anglos (Dieppa, 1977).

While corresponding figures for elderly Cubans are not available, Szapocznik, et al., (1977) finds that, because most older Cubans were forced to leave their homeland as political exiles, they were stripped of all financial resources. Their economic situation in concert with their advanced age made it difficult for them to launch or resume remunerative careers. This radical revision of financial status from their situation in Cuba (in which elders usually own most family-held resources and properties) has made life in the U.S. extremely traumatic for older Cuban immigrants. These circumstances make it unlikely that older Cubans have been any more able than other Hispanics to accumulate significant personal savings.

4. Mandated Transfer Payments

Because older Hispanics have too few sources of financial support, they are overrepresented in populations of persons receiving supplemental Social Security Income (SSI). In Cantor's sample of older Puerto Ricans in New York City (1976), 45 percent were receiving SSI, in contrast with 9 percent of the white sample. While elderly Mexican Americans were also more likely to be receiving welfare than were older Anglos, they used these programs far less often than older Puerto Ricans. As Valle and Mendoza (1978) report, only 7 percent of their elderly Mexican-American sample received welfare, while Dieppa (1977) found that only 6 percent of the Mexican Americans in her study in the Southwest were on welfare. Since so many elderly Hispanics are forced out of the labor market at a relatively young age because of poor health, one might expect them to turn to disability programs as a source of income until they became eligible for retirement benefits. Valle and Mendoza (1978), however, found that only 4 percent of elderly Mexican Americans in their study received disability benefits. Although many more older Hispanics could certainly use such assistance, the program's stringent definitions of disability make most Hispanics who have been

forced to retire early due to poor health ineligible for such benefits (McConnell, et al., 1979).

F. HEALTH AND MENTAL HEALTH

Health

The incidence and severity of health problems among the aged is well documented. Although data concerning levels of physical impairment among Hispanic elderly are limited, existing information suggests that older Mexicans and Puerto Ricans are more likely to suffer from physical impairments than their white counterparts. Ragan and Simonia (1977) show that 28 percent of elderly Chicanos rated their health as "poor" or "very poor", compared with four percent of older whites. Valle and Mendoza (1978) found a similar proportion (30%) of older Hispanics who reported that their health was poor. Among male retirees in Arizona and New Mexico, Dieppa (1977) found that white respondents were twice as likely as Mexican Americans to say they felt as healthy as they did when they were working. Older Puerto Ricans are also in poorer health than their non-Hispanic peers. While only one in four (23%) of Puerto Ricans in Cantor's (1976) study of elderly New York City residents said they were in good health, more than two-fifths (41%) of whites enjoyed good health. Such impairment can seriously affect the elders' ability to maintain themselves in the community. Newquist, et. al. (1979), for example, reports that older Mexican Americans were twice as likely as older whites to have impairments which prevent them from shopping or attending social or church functions. Moreover, two out of three (64%) older Chicanos, in contrast with two out of five (42%) older whites said poor health prevented them from holding a regular job. Cantor and Meyer (1976) report that almost two-thirds (62%) of the older Puerto Ricans in their study in New York City were physically impaired, as opposed to less than half (48%) of the older white respondents.

Clark (1979) and Cantor (1976) both found that the health of elderly urban residents is generally worse than their rural counterparts. Their results were corroborated by Korte's (1978) research on urban and rural Hispanics in New Mexico. There he found only 19 percent of rural repondents, in contrast with 52 percent of urban respondents, who said their health was "poor" or "very poor".

Poor health and related limitations in functioning are not only more prevalent among older Mexican Americans and Puerto Ricans than Anglos, but the onset of health problems is earlier among older Hispanics than whites. This may explain why Mexican Americans die younger than Anglos. The average life expectancy of Mexican Americans was 56.7 years in 1960, compared with 67.5 for whites (Bengston, et. al., 1977). Sanchez (1974) believes a 48 year-old Hispanic migrant is at about the same level of health as a 65 year-old Anglo. Newquist, et al., (1979) found that one-third (33%) of Los Angeles Mexican Americans between the ages of 45 and 50 compared with 5 percent of white respondents in the same age category have health problems impairing their ability to work. Data from the same survey also show that the aging process magnifies existing health differences between younger Hispanics and Anglos. Hispanics in poorer health at middle-age were more impaired than whites in old age. Perceived health status declined by 19 percent from middle to old age among Hispanics, while the fall among whites was only 9 percent. Health differences between Hispanics and whites are directly correlated with socioeconomic differences. More Mexican Americans than Anglos, for example, are manual laborers and work in other physically taxing jobs which involve debilitating work conditions. These harsh conditions are associated with early retirement due to poor health (Cantor, 1976; Newquist et al., 1979; Newton, 1980). Cantor and Meyer (1976) found that among older residents of New York City, income was the best predictor of health status, overshadowing other factors such as ethnicity, sex, or living arrangements. While a strong relationship between income and health also was observed by Newquist, et al. (1979), elderly Mexican Americans as a group were still three times more likely than Anglos in the same income group to have poor health; therefore, the differences in income do not fully explain the relative poor health of older Mexican Americans as compared with Anglos (Newquist, et al., 1979). Perhaps these differences are exacerbated by failure to adopt a preventive health orientation or lack of adequate health care in or near Hispanic communities.

Health Service Utilization

Barriers to the use of services probably confront Hispanic elderly and contribute to their underuse of particular types of services. Some of these barriers are cultural. Older Hispanics may shy away from using highly technological, depersonalized systems of modern medical care because these services fail to meet the medical expectations, attitudes, and needs of Hispanics who are used to more personal, family-oriented medical settings and care.

Older Mexican Americans have been described in research as preferring a caretaker-patient relationship characterized by personalismo wherein individuals relate to each other as persons, and treat each other with respeto (respect), dignidad (dignity), delicadeza (gentleness), and comprension (understanding) (Newton, 1980; Sotomayor, 1973; Valle and Mendoza, 1978). Therefore, not surprisingly, the impersonal and contractual service provider-patient relationship of the public health-care system alienates older Hispanics (Solis, 1975). From the moment they are processed into a hospital or health clinic, older Hispanics are made painfully aware of the inferior role to which they are relegated. Because they lack education and are unfamiliar with service delivery institutions, they feel alienated. Hispanic elders often have difficulty understanding and filling out forms, and the authoritarian and bureaucratic role of service providers is frequently threatening.

Considerations of cost, availability and access to health-care, also act as barriers to medical care for elderly Hispanics. Cantor and Meyer (1976) found, for example, that income rather than ethnicity had the greatest predictive value concerning use of health-care services by inner-city elderly. The poorest of the three ethnic groups studied, inner-city Puerto Ricans, used services least often. Approximately 64 percent of older members of this group, in contrast to 37 percent of older whites, cited lack of money as one reason they did not go to a doctor when ill (Cantor and Meyer, 1976).

Health-insurance programs designed to protect the elderly from the high cost of medical care also are unable to provide adequate economic coverage for low-income older Hispanics. Medicare covers only about 40 percent of the total health costs and does not cover the cost of eyeglasses, hearing aids, or dental care (Newquist, et al., 1979). Because their work was less-stable and less-remunerative, they are less likely than whites to be eligible for Social Security, older Hispanics are also less likely than Anglos to be covered by Medicare (Crouch, 1972). In Southern California, Newquist, et al., (1979) found that among the 60-to-64-year-old cohort, 21 percent of Mexican Americans, as contrasted with 12 percent of whites, lacked health insurance of any kind.

Cantor and Meyer (1976) documented ethnic disparities in utilization patterns. Four-fifths (80%) of older white respondents in their survey patronized private physicians, while older Puerto Ricans were only half as likely to do so. In contrast, half (50%) of the older Puerto Ricans used hospital outpatient clinics for health services, and they were twice as likely as whites to have been hospitalized.

Lack of access to medical services is also a problem for older Hispanics. Older Puerto Ricans cited transportation-related problems twice as often as older whites as a reason for not seeking a physician when ill. Almost half (46%) said medical facilities were located too far away, and two of every five (40%) said they had no one to take them there when they were ill (Cantor and Meyer, 1976). For these reasons older Hispanics may wait until they are seriously ill before seeking medical treatment. This delayed use of services may also explain why Cantor and Meyer (1976) found that older Puerto Ricans are twice as likely as older whites to have been hospitalized.

"Folk Medicine"

Research on the use of folk healers such as "curanderos" and "espiritistas" and of folk-curing practices is more germane to discussions

29

of health among elder persons than it is in assessing health practices among younger cohorts of Hispanics (Sotomayor, 1973). However, it would be misleading to assume that the perceptions of illness and healing espoused by the majority of older Hispanics are determined by folk beliefs. According to Newton (1980), cultural orientations vary greatly by region, and traditional medical beliefs and practices are much more prevalent among elderly Chicanos in rural south Texas than among those in urban Southern California. This contention is supported by Keefe, et al.'s (1979) finding that only 7 percent of Chicanos in their Southern California study had ever used the services of a "curandero".

Mental Health

The Concept of Aging

A number of researchers suggest the terms "mental health" and "mental illness" must be redefined to reflect the sociocultural context in which they occur (Korte, 1978). Newton and Ruiz (1981) believe the mental health of elderly Mexican Americans should be viewed in terms of their "adjustment to aging." This construct would include both psychological and sociohistorical dimensions such as perceptions of aging, life satisfaction, the Hispanic community and the dominant society within which it is embedded, and primary group support. Such an approach to assessing mental health not only avoids the difficulties of measuring symptoms of mental health by measuring comparative differences between ethnic groups, but also provides information which can be used to help devise alternative methods of service delivery to reverse the current pattern of underuse of mental health services by Hispanics.

Researchers on Hispanic gerontology agree that Mexican Americans perceive the onset of old-age as occurring earlier than do Anglos. In Los Angeles, 30 percent of Mexican-American respondents considered themselves old by age 57, while the same proportion of Anglos did not consider themselves old until age 70 (Bengtson, et al., 1977). Similarly, Crouch (1972) found in West Texas that two-thirds of Hispanics there felt old-age begins before 60, while 45 percent said it begins between 50 and 55. Only 8 percent of Mexican Americans said the onset of old-age is at 65, the age at which persons are eligible for full benefits or government assistance programs. In East Los Angeles, the belief that old-age begins before 60 is reflected in the participation of barrio residents in voluntary organizations for Senior Citizens at relatively early ages (Cuellar, 1978).

Researchers have suggested a number of reasons for this perception. Newton and Ruiz (1981) associate Mexican Americans' perception of the early onset of old-age with their early onset of poor health. Crouch (1972) believes old-age comes early for Mexican Americans because they associate it with the end of the work role. Since they labor in physically demanding jobs, they often must leave the work force relatively early due to the passing of their physical prime. Newton and Ruiz (1981), however, feel the end of working roles is an indirect indicator of poor health. Markides (1980) found some support for the idea that persons in poorer health are more likely than others to believe old-age comes earlier in life. In this comparative study of elderly whites and Chicanos in San Antonio, the strongest variable associated with self-identification as elderly was the respondent's chronological age. The respondents' levels of education also appeared to have a significant effect on their age identification. The less education they had, the more likely they were to identify themselves as old at an early age.

Ethnicity also entered the equation. Mexican Americans of comparable ages to whites, more often viewed themselves as being old. Markides (1980) suggested that this finding reflects that since older Mexican Americans do not attach such a negative connotation to old-age, they are less likely to deny it than elderly whites. However, this explanation is questionable since other studies on the prevailing orientation among Hispanics towards aging show they view aging no more positively than do Anglos. In West Texas, Crouch (1972) learned that more than half the Mexican Americans (55%) there felt old-age was, on the whole, undesirable. Only 13 percent saw old-age in a positive light. Ragan (1978) discovered that similar percentages of whites and Mexican Americans viewed aging positively; but when asked how they felt about their own ages, Mexican Americans over 65 were only half as likely as their white or Black counterparts to express positive feelings about growing old.

It is unclear why Hispanics are likely to regard old-age more negatively than members of other ethnic groups. More research may help determine whether the pessimism results from a realistic assessment of the quality of life in old-age, from a cultural predisposition, or from an ethnically related artifact in survey research which prompts Hispanics to respond differently to questions on the topic.

Attitudes Toward Death

Although older Mexican Americans may be more pessimistic about old-age than their white counterparts, existing studies on the perception of the future and attitudes toward death indicate they are no more likely than older whites to fear death or dwell on the topic. Bengtson, et al., (1977) and Reynolds and Kalish (1974) both report older Mexican Americans are no more likely than elderly whites to fear death. Both studies also find that older members of all ethnic groups are much less likely than middle-age persons to fear death. However, Mexican Americans in Los Angleles generally expected to die sooner than did either whites or Blacks (Bengtson, et al. 1977). This finding was not supported in Reynolds and Kalish's (1974) survey in which ethnic differences concerning expected longevity were insignificant among white and Hispanic respondents.

Acculturation

Szapocznik et al. (1978) believe acculturation is a complex process involving two distinct dimensions: adoption of the host society's behavioral norms (language, habits, and life style) and adoption of the host culture's value orientation. Both of these aspects affect the psychological well-being of older Hispanics.

Because use of the English language is cited as a key indicator of acculturation, elderly Hispanics who generally prefer to use their native Spanish are considered to be minimally acculturated into the Anglo-American culture. According to Sanchez (1975), use of Spanish is relatively high among all ages of Hispanics. He finds one out of every two Hispanics living in the U.S. speaks Spanish at home. This figure rises to 72 percent among Puerto Ricans, and goes to 87 percent among Cubans. Use of the Spanish language is even more prevalent among older Hispanics. Virtually all older Cuban residents of Miami, for instance, used the Spanish language; almost none used English (Szapocznik, et al., 1978). More than four out of five (84%) of those elderly Latinos preferred to use the Spanish language, while only one in three (37%) felt confident in expressing themselves in written English. Thirty percent did not speak English.

A number of authors believe the continued use of the Spanish language contributes to the low level of social integration of elderly Hispanics into the Anglo-American culture. Szapocznik et al. (1977) went one step further when they stated that the language exacerbates difficulties associated with adapting to old age because Hispanics are less likely to know about and use health and social service programs for the elderly. Sotomayor (1971) agrees that the use of Spanish isolates Hispanic elders from the Anglo's culture, but believes it is possible that this isolation has psychological benefits. By insulating older Hispanics from negative messages and discrimination coming from the dominant society, the use of Spanish may protect older Hispanics from psychological distress. Also, because the use of Spanish separates those who use it from members of the dominant Anglo culture, the use of Spanish may reinforce the bonds that unite members of Hispanic communitites (Sotomayor, 1971).

Levels of Interaction

Traditionally, older Hispanics lived in extended families where their advanced age was regarded with respect, and wherein they had specific social roles to perform. Filling these culturally determined family roles maintained their feelings of self-worth and self-confidence, and had a positive effect on their mental health. However, as Szapocznik et al. (1978) point out, these family traditions are weakened as family members become more and more acculturated into the Anglo way of life. Because younger persons acculturate more rapidly than older persons, and differences in acculturation between age groups cause interpersonal conflict, lives of older Hispanics are likely to become more and more distressful as traditional family patterns are disrupted.

While Szapocznik, et al., (1978) focus on the deleterious effects of these intergenerational differences in acculturation between adolescents and their parents, their data indicate the gap between older adults and middle-aged respondents is even more pronounced. This suggests that older adults may experience the severest degree of alienation from the cultural values and behavior of their adult offspring and from the society in which they live.

Both Korte (1978) and Nunez(1977) emphasize the importance of normative expectations of familial interaction for maintaining morale among Chicano elderly. Nunez shows that older Mexican Americans have greater expectations concerning familial interaction than do respondents of other ethnicities. Consequently, Nunez predicts that unmet expectations of family interaction will have more deleterious effects upon older Mexican Americans than upon older Anglos (Nunez, 1977). Korte's (1978) study indicates urbanization often has negative effects upon the morale of older Hispanics because there is less kin interaction among city dwellers than among rural residents. Among Chicanos, older rural couples showed significantly higher levels of both morale and kin interaction than did elderly couples who were urban residents.

Friendships and mutual help from barrio residents may take the place of family interaction for older Hispanics confronted with the dissolution of familial networks due to rapid acculturation of younger cohorts of Hispanics living in nuclear families. Sotomayor (1980) characterizes the barrio as a social arena in which interaction is characterized by mutual helping networks, in which people come together in order to gain a sense of security, and in which needs produced by a shared tradition of cultural customs and heritage can be fulfilled. Moreover living in supportive ethnic communities can reduce stress caused by migration, especially if the host society displays negative prejudices which tend to add to a migrant's feelings of insecurity and anxiety. Cuellar (1978) and Korte (1978) also cite examples of adaptation to the loss of traditional forms of morale-building through social interaction among older Hispanic barrio residents.

That the quality of neighborhood life is important to life satisfaction of older urban Chicanos is also supported by Korte's (1978) finding that the only elderly respondents who had high levels of morale, despite lowered levels of kin interaction, were those who had successfully substituted interaction with neighbors for interaction with kin. Cuellar (1978) links the rapid proliferation of senior citizen's clubs in the East

Los Angeles barrio, a social form not found in traditional Mexican society, as proof of the need for new social settings in which elderly Chicanos can develop interpersonal relationships. Cuellar feels membership in voluntary organizations can help older Hispanics learn new social roles and develop relationships that will permit them to demonstrate their social competence and thereby generate prestige and self-esteem. Thus, senior citizen's clubs can help fill the psychological and social void left when traditional roles, values, and expectations, associated with aging no longer exist in the urban, nontraditional setting of the host society.

SUMMARY AND CONCLUSIONS

There is a paucity of published research focusing on the conditions and needs of Hispanic elders. However, the available work suggests that ethnicity, cultural characteristics, and socioeconomic status are related both to the physical health and to the psychic well-being of Hispanic elders. For example, Hispanics become "old" at an earlier age and have a shorter life expectancy than Anglos. This is attributable, at least in part, to the demands of hard physical labor, low financial remuneration, and those factors affected by economics such as poor housing, poor sanitation conditions, and poor health, as well as the concomitant psychological impairment that arises from these circumstances. Although it is difficult to measure the impact of psychological variables on life expectancy, certainly isolation, alienation, and depression cannot be conducive to extending life.

The respected role that the older person has traditionally held in the extended family is conflicting with the highly independent lifestyles of Hispanic children and grandchildren fostered by American urban culture. The difficulty that Hispanic elders have in adapting to these sudden changes in their cultural milieu has contributed to a greater incidence of mental health problems.

In general, the Hispanic elder suffers from poor health, lives in substandard housing and sanitation conditions, is financially depressed, is faced with the disruption of traditional values and norms, and has access to few services that focus on his or her needs. While Hispanic elders are growing in numbers, they may be becoming more isolated from their traditional ties.

Research to date on the Hispanic elder has been limited; however, from that which does exist, the following conclusions may be drawn.

1. The Hispanic population is quickly becoming the largest minority group in the United States, with high concentrations in urban areas. Specifically, the Hispanic elderly population is rapidly increasing.

34

2. Mexican Americans experience special problems related to immigration to the United States without legal status. These problems are closely related to sociocultural issues of lower-class status, discrimination, and acculturation.

3. Problems associated with biculturalism are especially pronounced for Hispanics because of the close geographical proximity of Hispanic and Anglo-American cultures.

4. Changing cultural values are creating a generation gap between young and old Hispanics. Elders find it difficult to replace informal, extended family supports as the forces of modernization erode traditional values.

5. Hispanic elders suffer from a very high level of depression as the erosion of traditional cultural values associated with family and work leave them without a meaningful role in society.

6. Problems associated with growing older are greatly exacerbated in the Hispanic population by poverty, cultural alienation, and language barriers.

7. The low socioeconomic status of many Hispanic elders, primarily attributable to unskilled, hard labor employment, results in conditions associated with poverty. These include: poor health, inadequate health care, inadequate housing, and insufficient retirement income.

8. Private sector involvement and governmental assistance have generally failed to be sensitive to and responsive to the unique problems of Hispanic elders.

9. The modern "leisure ethic" in America is not compatible with the "work ethic" and lifestyle of Hispanic elders in their retirement years.

10. Cultural barriers, language barriers, and limited availability of services impede access to needed services by Hispanic elders.

CHAPTER II

HISPANIC RESEARCH CONSIDERED

The current body of knowledge about the conditions and problems faced by Hispanic elders shows that past discrimination and limited educational resources have restricted Hispanics to low-income, hard-labor jobs, providing little or no retirement savings. Many are forced to retire early because of the overtaxing demands of strenuous labor (Newton, 1980). Many Hispanics perceive themselves as old earlier than other groups (Bengtson and Ragan, 1977), suffer from illnesses related to poverty, malnutrition, and inadequate medical care (Bell, et al. 1976), and perceive old age as undesirable (Crouch, 1972).

In terms of culture and society, Hispanic elders often feel they do not fit. Many are caught between traditional cultural values which emphasize the importance of family and the respected position of elders, and the values which emphasize the nuclear family, which tends to be highly mobile and removed from close contact with the extended family. As a result, Hispanic elders have found themselves alone and isolated in a "foreign culture" without sufficient social, emotional or economic supports. Their uncertain command of the English language undermines the self-confidence they need to aggressively seek out and obtain social and medical services. In effect, they are placed in double jeopardy. Their low-income position in society leaves them without adequate resources, while cultural and linguistic barriers restrict their use of available services thereby compounding their problems (Bengtson, 1979).

More research is necessary and is likely to be undertaken in this decade to more fully elucidate the conditions, problems and needs confronting the Hispanic elderly. Those who construct the new research efforts should carefully consider the lessons of the past. This chapter addresses those methodological issues and research problems which should be considered in future work on Hispanics and specifically, the Hispanic elderly. While much can be gleaned from current research literature, little has been published that specifically addresses research in a Hispanic community and population. This chapter incorporated the experiences of Hispanic researchers currently engaged in relevant research, the contributions of the experts gathered to participate in this project of evaluating Hispanic Gerontological Research and the extensive experience of the principal investigators for that Project. Thus, some of the methods cited will be contradictory because they are based on numerous viewpoints; however, they should provide worthwhile avenues of consideration. Most of the research identified is based upon surveys, thus the focus is on this type of design; however, other research designs are also addressed in this overview.

37

A. THE RESEARCHER AND THE RESEARCHED

The Researcher

A current controversy in Hispanic research concerns the issue of who is the best qualified to do research in Hispanic communities. As more Hispanics become trained in research skills, the excuse that there are "no qualified Hispanics" becomes invalid and no longer a viable excuse for not engaging Hispanics in research efforts. The question however, still remains, "who is best qualified?"

Today the study of the Hispanic elderly is criticized because previous, mostly Anglo researchers failed to include or be sensitive to cultural issues in their research methodologies. These failures have often been attributed to unconscious racism, cultural bias, or lack of sufficient knowledge about cultural differences. For example, until the 1960's, the "melting pot" or "assimilationist school" dominated social science. It held that racial and ethnic groups ultimately lose their separate ways of life. The normative American way of life drew the major focus of social science research, serving as the standard against which racial and ethnic groups were studied (Yin, 1973).

Because the minority population perceives non-minority researchers as having failed in the past to understand meaningfully the plight of minorities, Anglo researchers are viewed with great skepticism. In fact, one avenue of work today in minority research is to analyze critically the scientific rigor of some of the earlier cross-cultural research, and to address issues of cultural bias and unsubstantiated research findings. A few non-minority researchers have undertaken the task of criticizing others' works as well as their own in the interest of improving the methodology of minority research and ensuring the quality and credibility of their findings (Rainwater and Yancy, 1967; Blauner and Wellman, 1973; Moore, 1973; Staples, 1976; Trimble, 1977).

Despite all this, the primary question still needs to be addressed. The three most commonly held points of view are: 1) all research on Hispanics should be conducted by Hispanics, 2) all research on Hispanics should be conducted by non-Hispanics, and 3) Hispanic research should be conducted by those best able to carry it out in an effective and efficient manner. As detailed in the following pages, all three approaches have advantages and disadvantages.

1. All research on Hispanics should be conducted by Hispanics

The major advantage to having Hispanics conduct research on Hispanics is the presence of an assumed cultural sensitivity and understanding of cultural norms and language. This can provide insight into both the conceptualization of research questions and objectives, and the analyses and interpretation of the data. To insure that such insights are used to their best advantage, specific subgroups could be matched to specific geographical area. For instance, Cuban researchers familiar with the Cuban community in Florida could conduct research there, or Mexican-American researchers familiar with the Mexican-American community in California could conduct research there. The Hispanic researcher brings a perspective and understanding that cannot be taught, a perspective gained primarily from life experiences. In this respect, there is no substitute for first-hand knowledge.

The disadvantage to this approach is that one who has experienced or lives close to the people being researched is often the least able to make a critical, objective appraisal of the situation. Additionally, the criterion of Hispanic background is frequently no assurance of cultural understanding or sensitivity. Through the process of schooling to obtain research skills, a particular type of acculturation takes place that may set the Hispanic researcher apart from the community he or she is researching, thus making the researcher a reflection of his or her Anglo counterparts.

In spite of the disadvantages, proponents of this view feel that it is preferable, since it provides greater assurance of cultural sensitivity, credibility, and access to the community. The disadvantages, however, must be acknowledged, and they ultimately make any strict adherence to this approach, while desirable, untenable.

2. All research on Hispanics should be conducted by non-Hispanics

The major argument for having research on Hispanics conducted by non-Hispanics is the objectivity that can be maintained by those who stand outside of the culture. Additionally, many non-Hispanics are well-versed in Hispanic culture and language, and are thus able to provide both the sensitivity and objectivity necessary to adequately reflect Hispanic needs. Furthermore, non-Hispanics who are not only trained in research skills, but also have experience in carrying out large-scale research efforts are much more readily available.

Obviously, these arguments have been used to support what has been the status quo in Hispanic research and the previous research, predominately conducted by non-Hispanics, has not, as viewed by Hispanic researchers today, reflected the Hispanic mind. Thus, this approach is inadequate.

3. Hispanic research should be conducted by those best able to carry it out in an effective and efficient manner

Neither of the first two approaches are possible or valid in the real world, nor should they be. Unfortunately, no criteria can be given for "who is best able" or "an effective and efficient manner." These are subjective judgments, based on the particular research to be pursued, the needs of the project, the skills of the participants, and any other criteria deemed necessary to fulfill the research goal. There are, however, some guidelines that Hispanic researchers suggest should be considered in the preliminary planning stages of any research that will include a Hispanic population.

Recommendations:

a) Any research focusing on Hispanics should be headed by a Hispanic familiar with the language, the culture and the geographical areas of the specific subgroup or at least one subgroup, as well as the content of the topic. If this is not possible, the non-Hispanic heading the research must be sensitive to and understanding of issues concerning Hispanics, and must employ a Hispanic in a position to influence the research effort, or at least to provide collaboration and feedback.

b) Research that is not necessarily Hispanic-focused, but will include a Hispanic subsample, should employ Hispanics to aid in the development of the instruments, to ensure linguistic and conceptual equivalence, and to aid in the analyses and interpretation of the data as it pertains to the Hispanic.

c) Project participants at every level of the investigation should be selected based upon the knowledge and sensitivity toward and about Hispanic cultures.

The Researched

The community, or those researched, have resented researchers who seek to use communities as a laboratory, but provide little in exchange. As a result, institutions involved in the funding, execution, and application of social science research have been forced to acknowledge a new constituency to whom they are accountable: the community being researched.

The criticisms leveled against the traditional methods of social science inquiry conducted in minority settings challenged the findings resulting from such studies on the grounds that they were conceptually, methodologically, and ethically unacceptable. The most salient criticisms voiced by representatives of minority communities can be summarized as follows:

- Research is done to advance the career of the researcher rather than to develop information that could benefit the minority community.

- Researchers do not perceive themselves as having any accountability to research subjects.

40

- Researchers' findings have often been harmful to the minority community, portraying behavior patterns as pathological. This contributes to stereotyping and undermines the need for social services; it also rationalizes social inequities by blaming the victims for their circumstances.

- Research monies would be better spent funding direct service programs to ameliorate the plight of those in need (Ragan, 1973; Bengston, 1979).

Minority community representatives have developed considerable sophistication in making reticent or even hostile academic researchers recognize them as legitimate participants in the research process. At times they have refused to submit to interviewing, or appealed directly to funding agencies to gain recognition for their concerns.

The experiences of researchers working in Hispanic communities are varied. Community member participation in research can range from nominal to collegial. Bengtson et al. (1977), referring to the community problems encountered in the University of Southern California Cultural Contexts of Aging Study counsels researchers not to be naive about the potential power of community groups, to build community involvement into the research process, and to adapt a flexible stance to facilitate conflict resolution. It should be noted, however, that the noninvolvement of minority researchers at the inception of the project, as has been previously recommended, was one major contributing factor to the turmoil faced by the USC study, and is still at issue in the interpretation of the study's findings.

Weiss' (1977) survey of research studies done in poor communities indicates that the majority of the researchers sampled did make some provision for the involvement of community leaders or members of community advisory panels in the study. While there was substantial consensus on the rationale behind involving community members in the research project, the researchers' stated motives were pragmatic, overwhelmingly to "get the job done." There was less agreement on the role that community persons were to assume within the project. Weiss found that researchers most commonly used community leaders or advisory panel members to promote acceptance of the study in the community, and to aid the recruitment of staff personnel, including interviewers. Less frequently mentioned was the involvement of community representatives in collegial roles, such as in planning the study and in interpreting and disseminating study findings.

As with the issue of "who should conduct Hispanic research," there are three points of view on the issue of involving the community in research efforts: 1) always involve the community in the research in some way, 2) never involve the community in the research unless the research cannot be carried out without their input, and 3) the decision to involve the community members and the degree of involvement should be dictated by the research concerns.

Rather than outline each argument, advantages and disadvantages of community involvement will be addressed, and particular types of involvement will be explained in detail.

If, as previously recommended, a Hispanic researcher has been employed, the community involvement issue is likely to be managed with greater ease. This is primarily because the employing of a Hispanic who is sensitive to cultural issues will already suggest cognizance of community concerns, or at least that the project may be better able to respond to them as the research progresses. Many of the problems regarding community involvement arise from lack of any similar ethnic or social representation on projects.

There are many distinct advantages to involving the community, including the following:

1. Gaining access. It is often necessary to gain entry to communities, especially those that are ethnically homogeneous and enclosed by particular boundaries. Strangers are easily spotted in these areas and they require legitimization, otherwise the research may be faced with a high degree of suspicion, low response rate, large degree of missing data, and inaccurate information. In some cases, researchers have even encountered physical violence after entering areas where they were perceived as outsiders.

One may engage the community as a participant to increase access in several ways: gain the sponsorship of an ethnic voluntary or community service agency well known in the area; explain the purpose of the research to a variety of appropriate groups such as church groups, community agencies, and social groups; train indigenous personnel to participate in the study as interviewers, listers, screeners, or in some other staff capacity; or publicly announce the scope and purpose of the research through the mass media.

2. Developing the Instrument. No one knows the community structure, behavioral patterns, linguistic patterns, subgroup differences, or sensitive areas better than those the research will address. In this respect, community members may act as consultants for the development of the questionnaire, as translators from one language to the other (English to Spanish and vice versa), or as persons to aid in reliability and validity testing. The reliability and validity testing function might, for instance, be carried out by a community panel.

3. Recruitment, Training, and Interviewing. Community agencies are an excellent source of assistance for identifying potential interviewers. Moreover, if training can be conducted at one of the

agencies or community centers, it will engage the community and curtail travel time for community members who participate in the training. In short, community agencies can help with recruiting, training, and interviewing.

4. <u>Data Analysis and Interpretation</u>. It is often useful to elicit community members' help in providing a more accurate interpretation of the findings since meanings attached to particular concepts or events may be best understood in that community context.

5. <u>Disseminating Findings</u>. The community usually is unaware of the outcome of many of the studies conducted on them, and yet community members are often interested. Brief summaries can be distributed, oral reports can be made to community groups and agencies, or reports can be made available to interested individuals and groups. In the Hispanic community, word-of-mouth is the most powerful dissemination tool available.

While all of the above are possible ways of involving the community of the researched in a project, these methods are not always fruitful or advantageous. Some problems may arise as a result of the internal politics of communities. Opposing factions within communities may create conflict detrimental to the research effort by placing the researcher in the midst of community turmoil. Additionally, the time spent in community contacts may not justify the minimal gains.

Recently, it has become fashionable to select interviewers from the community; this also may not be fruitful. Matching interviewers and respondents by ethnicity and language should be standard practice in survey research, but it may not always be best to recruit from the specific geographical areas being studied. Familiarity with respondents often jeopardizes the reliability of responses; people may not want to provide personal information to someone from the same community. Or, the interviewer may feel that some questions are too personal to ask; so he or she will not probe, and then accepts the first response given which may be "don't know."

Weiss (1977) assessed interview performance in a comparison between indigenous, race-matched, and non-matched interviewers. Performance in twelve task areas were noted, including establishing rapport with respondents, locating hard-to-reach respondents, following interview specifications, asking questions as they appear on the schedule, recording answers, doing interviews punctually, reporting to the supervisor, and submitting forms promptly. Study directors rated indigenous interviewers highest on only one task: establishing rapport with respondents. Indigenous interviewers also rated well in comparison with race-matched and non-matched interviewers on one other task: locating hard-to-reach respondents. On all other tasks, non-matched interviewers, usually middle-class whites, were rated highest and indigenous interviewers were rated lowest. The lack of previous experience in interviewing seems to have been one of the primary reasons for low performance ratings among indigenous interviewers. In the cases where indigenous interviewers had previous experiences, their ratings were close to, and sometimes surpassed, the ratings of non-matched interviewers. Thus, the training of indigenous interviewers becomes critical if they are to be selected and used.

Moore (1979) successfully linked the academic world and the community by making the researched the researcher in the study, Homeboys. Although that effort took time, it was necessary to achieve the goals of the research.

Thus, whether to involve the community in a research project, to what degree they should be involved, what specific roles can they undertake, all these issues can be evaluated only in light of the researcher's own skills, the needs of the project, the needs of the community, and the desired outcome of the research. Again, a set policy of always or never involving the community will invariably result in difficulties, while the middle ground speaks to needs and goals of both the researcher and the researched.

B. RESEARCH DESIGN

Different research methods exist because they are useful for addressing different research questions about populations of varying sizes. Are you interested in examining a few cases in depth or many cases in less depth? Are you interested in what people report, or do you seek the evidence that documents what they actually do? As we attempt to identify problems, assess needs, improve social services, understand behavior, or describe processes, we must ask ourselves, "Which type of research method and design best serves the objective?"

The two major designs, used with variation in methods are the ethnographic approach and the survey approach. While all the instruments included in this report were used in surveys, they all could be enhanced by the addition of one of the ethnographic techniques. Thus, while time and cost constraints often prohibit the use of both, the gains made by the combination of both must be given serious consideration, particularly in researching minority communities. The impact of culture is difficult to assess without these combined methods, for one provides greater opportunity to generalize while the other allows for closer inspection of detail. Thus, researchers should be able to gain by blending survey methodology with ethnographic or field research techniques when conducting research in the Hispanic community.

Because of the wide range of ethnographic designs, including in-depth interviews, life histories, geneology, participant observation, unobtrusive measures, the extended case method, and social network analysis, we will not undertake a comprehensive taxonomy of the numerous methodological hybrids which have resulted from the cross-fertilization

44

of survey and ethnographic techniques. Instead, the focus will be on the ethnographic adaptations to survey research that are readily employable. These fall into three general categories: 1) the use of ethnographic techniques to generate concepts and hypotheses as a preliminary to traditional survey research techniques, 2) the use of indigenous informants to help analyze and draw inferences from survey data, and 3) the use of ethnographically derived interview techniques such as the in-depth interview. The common denominator among all of these methodological hybrids is their emphasis on the establishment of rapport and the formation of closer ties with the research subjects than are usually cultivated in standard survey techniques, an approach more commonly associated with the field methods of anthropology.

Participant observation is the basis for all other ethnographic methods; it provides the insights from which other measures can be developed. Its primary characteristic, close involvement with research subjects, permits the generation of concepts, hypotheses, and unanticipated data which can be especially important as a preliminary phase of survey research. In addition to yielding pretest information which can improve the survey instrument, fieldwork often provides a means of gaining legitimacy for the survey (Seiber, 1973). Had participant observation been the norm as the preliminary phase of minority community survey research, many of the charges levied against urban sociologists in the mid-'60's, such as aloofness from research subjects and invalid conceptual and analytical frameworks for research, might have been avoided.

Cuellar (1974) cites the use of ethnographic methods in conjunction with survey techniques in the USC Cultural Contexts of Aging Study. Ethnographic research complimented the community survey component of the overall research project by generating empirically-based concepts and salient topics for possible inclusion in the survey instrument. In-depth interview techniques were also used as a pre-test to generate categories of forced-choice responses, and to elicit qualitative responses which would compliment information generated through the forced choice questionnaire items.

The use of indigenous information as an adjunct to traditional survey methodology has, in the case of research in minority communities, often been done through community representative panels working with the researcher in an advisory capacity. In her survey of research study directors, Weiss (1977) found that about a quarter of the researchers surveyed formed advisory committees to work with their study. Of these, 22% involved the community group in planning the study, and 10% reported that the community representatives assisted the research staff in interpreting the findings. Ostensibly, the involvement of community representatives in these activities serves the same purpose as cited earlier for participant observation: namely, to generate an appropriate conceptual framework within which hypotheses are formulated, tested, and the resultant data interpreted to produce findings.

45

However, the relationship between minority community advisory committees and researchers can be so highly charged that the advisory role can be eclipsed by political agendas. If a community panel is to serve in an advisory capacity, their role and function should be clearly defined and agreed upon.

The most radical merging of ethnographic and survey research methodologies is marked by the abandonment of the forced choice questionnaire, substituting instead a combination of participant observation and in-depth interview. The in-depth interview can be as structured as an open-ended questionnaire or as unstructured as a directed conversation. In conjunction with more traditional survey techniques, such open-ended responses can aid in the interpretation and validation of survey data, as well as provide illustrative case-study material (Sieber, 1973). By itself, the in-depth interview demands rigorous quality control in the selection, training, and debriefing of interviewers in order to produce valid quantifiable data.

The rationale for use of the in-depth interview instead of survey techniques is based upon the belief that the inherent weaknesses of standard survey methodology make it unsuitable for use with respondents who are poor or of racial or ethnic minority backgrounds, or when the degree of social distance between researcher and respondent is very great (Myers, 1977). Proponents of the in-depth interview state that in such situations the rigid role prescriptions typical of standard survey procedures are ill-equipped to guide interviewers to gather valid responses. They feel that both attempts by respondents to resist and evade the interviewers, and de facto role violations on the part of respondents and interviewers will distort the findings.

The issue of de facto violation is frequently mentioned in the literature in conjunction with the elderly. Survey researchers in the field of gerontology commonly report problems involving false assumptions about interviewer-respondent relationships on the part of elderly respondents. From the respondent's point of view, it seems quite natural to treat the interviewer as a guest, expressing hospitality with gifts or insisting that the interviewer stay for a meal, often as an alternative to completing the interview (Kahana and Felton, 1977). The attitude implicit in traditional survey research is that false assumptions about interviewer-respondent relationships are not only time-consuming, and therefore costly, but that they also impinge on the dispassionate role of the interviewer which permits him to ask the respondent for personal or sensitive information with a minimum of interviewer effect on responses. In contrast to traditional survey research, which "corrects" false assumptions by imposing the role standards mandated by the researcher upon interviewer-respondent interaction, the ethnographic orientation to survey research attempt to modify the interview situation to meet both the researcher's need for information and the respondents' preferred mode of interaction.

46

Proponents of the in-depth interview as an alternative to traditional survey methods (Myers, 1977; Valle and Mendoza, 1978) state that the respondents' cultural expectations for interaction must be met if the interview is to be successful. Valle and Mendoza (1978), developers of La Platica interview technique, cite the need for bicultural expertise on the part of the interviewer, who must focus attention on the "interactional features of the intended relationship while remaining alert to the proper cues for moving ahead." Valle and Mendoza's survey of older Hispanics using La Platica methodology consists of a series of open questions which form the basis for a directed conversation. Interviewers were chosen from carefully screened bilingual, bicultural candidates, and subjected to weeks of training in the "culturally synchronous information gathering skills" embodied in La Platica methodology. Interviews, conducted at the respondent's home, took an average of four hours and included a formal introduction of the interviewer to the respondent by a third party "link person" from the respondent's community, a directed conversation which comprised the data-gathering portion of the interview, and, finally, a formal disengagement consisting of gift-giving or sharing a meal. Conversational responses were analyzed with the help of the interviewers to produce quantifiable data, an extremely time-consuming process in comparison with traditional survey techniques, and lacking the latter's capability to build-in tests for validity and reliability. The benefits of La Platica methodology outlined by Valle and Mendoza are: the researcher's ability to attain an enduring relationship to the studied community; the potential to develop future interventions such as service provision from these relationships; and the ability to trace the informal network of supportive resources available to the respondent population.

Ethnographic methodologies, which demand that the researcher become intimately involved with the population being researched, are intrinsically time intensive. However, these field methods are unsurpassed in their ability to provide illustrative and qualitative data about a population. The generation of this type of information plays a critical role in the preliminary development of effective survey research. All of the sources of this pretest information, such as receptivity, frame of reference and span of respondent attention, as well as salience and degree of inconclusiveness of survey instrument topics, can be considered under the rubric of qualitative field research (Sieber, 1973). Sources of this qualitative data include professional familiarity, exploratory participant observation, and indigenous informants. Of these sources, the latter two can serve the additional function of gaining legitimacy for the survey through contacts with community members.

Combining in-depth interview techniques (the open-ended question with forced-choice questions in a survey instrument) can provide a means of clarifying puzzling responses, validating the theoretical framework for the research, and validating findings by providing illustrative case-study information. However, the wholesale substitution of an in-depth interview format to provide quantifiable data is of questionable value. The drawbacks of methods such as La Platica are clear enough: they are time-consuming, expensive, and they demand highly trained and motivated indigenous interviewers to procure quantifiable data. The last requirement alone, considering the information developed by Weiss (1977) concerning indigenous interviewer job performance, would tend to make this methodology impractical. Furthermore, the benefits ascribed to this style of survey research are highly questionable. Valle and Mendoza's assertion that traditional survey methods are unsuitable for the Hispanic elderly is not supported by findings which indicate that non-response rates for elderly Latinos are among the lowest encountered in survey research (Dowd and Ragan, 1974). Although La Platica methodology is well suited to the formation of a long-lasting relationship between a researcher and a community, Valle and Mendoza's suggestion that this become the basis for future service-provision intervention has raised questions about violation of confidentiality in the minds of other researchers. Is it ethical to refer service providers to survey respondents on the basis of needs observed by or reported to interviewers (Kahana and Felton, 1977). The consequent lack of substantial benefits combined with the inherent difficulties of the in-depth interview as a substitute for traditional survey techniques suggest that less-radical hybrids of ethnographic and survey research techniques are of greater utility for research among the Hispanic elderly.

C. SURVEY ISSUES

Many topics pertain to the tasks involved in fielding a survey and most of these are covered in depth in a variety of textbooks on methods. However, three survey issues of particular importance for researchers of Hispanics are: sampling, questionnaire construction, and interviewer selection.

Sampling

Traditional surveys usually require that probabilistic sampling design be used to insure generalizability to the population being researched. While these designs are preferable in most cases, they are also very costly and time-consuming when the subject sought is characterized by a "rare trait". Using traditional areawide probability multi-stage sampling designs to locate subjects with rare traits can lead to enormous field time spent in screening potential respondents, thus extending data-collection periods beyond what is usually anticipated. For example, in a USC study of the elderly in Los Angeles County stratified by ethnicity, age cohorts, and social class, the sample selection and data collection time took approximately nine months to yield approximately 1200 completed interviews. Again in a Los Angeles study of Hispanic veterans a multi-stage probability design required that 11,000 households be screened to yield approximately 600 Hispanic veterans. These examples point out that traditional sampling methods used in surveys of subjects with unique characteristics will result in enormous expenditures of time, budget, and effort. Given the circumstances of time, budget and research goal, justification of this expense remains a matter of judgment.

What has apparently occurred to date is that the large studies of the elderly, using these traditional, expansive sampling designs, have yielded findings not much different from those using less-sophisticated sampling techniques. This is not to suggest that random-probability sampling should not be used whenever feasible, but rather that the researcher should not be wedded to one approach for fear that he or she will be criticized for lack of sophistication. All techniques should be considered as having equal viability. Perhaps for some circumstances, 95 percent confidence in the sample is unnecessary. It is with this in mind that the following points and suggestions are presented.

When the goal of the research is to investigate some facet of the lives of the Hispanic elderly, the researcher is focusing on a very small segment of the population. The Hispanic population is about 10 percent of the total population and within that group the older cohort constitutes about 10 percent of the Hispanic population. This is clearly sampling for a "rare trait."

To increase reliability, generalizability, and statistical-testing assumptions a combination of probability and nonprobability techniques are favored. Three common types of nonprobability designs can be merged with random-sampling techniques: purposive, dimensional, and snowball sampling.

Purposive or judgmental sampling is the selection of subjects based on the researcher's own judgment about which respondents best meet the purposes of the study. In constructing a purposive sampling frame of Hispanic elderly, the researcher should seek out other knowledgeable people to learn the location of the subjects. This could include leaders in the Hispanic community, community agencies, or other groups. A list of persons or geographical areas can be developed from which a random sample can be selected to generate the sample.

A purposive multistage sampling technique can be used by selecting specific geographical areas. For instance, the Hispanic elderly are more likely to gravitate towards areas of high Hispanic concentrations. Census tracts of areas populated by 50 percent or more Hispanics can constitute the sampling frame from which tracts can be randomly selected, and within that a random selection of blocks can be readily employed rather than random household selection. This is preferable since block coverage is more likely to yield greater numbers of elderly than household selection only.

Dimensional sampling is similar to purposive sampling, except that it specifies all the dimensions (variables) of interest. For example, with the elderly, representation of specific aged cohorts (55-64, 65-74, 75+), institutionalized and noninstitutionalized, and so forth, may be dimensions. In this example, there are six cells for which purposive samples can be generated and, if the groups are large enough, samples can be randomly selected. It approaches stratified sampling methods.

Snowball sampling has been used increasingly in recent years, particularly among researchers conducting community studies. TenHouten et al. (1971) have developed a strategy for using snowball sampling that allows for computation of estimates of sampling error and the use of statistical tests of significance. The term snowball sampling stems from the analogy of a snowball moving downhill and growing bigger and bigger. In the snowball sampling technique, each level of respondents provides the researcher with the next level of respondents until the desired sample size is achieved. In the first stage, a purposive sample of respondents is drawn. This can be done by selecting randomly from the purposive-sampling frame discussed earlier. This series of respondents act as informants to identify others who qualify for inclusion in the sample. From this set of perspective respondents, a random sample is drawn to form the next set of respondents and so on.

To be implemented with the greatest effectiveness, these sampling techniques require an understanding of Hispanic culture, the Hispanic elderly, and the community being researched. Additionally, these types of sampling designs are best incorporated into the research through the inclusion of some form of community support, as discussed in section A of this chapter, and the use of ethnomethodological techniques for preliminary work as discussed in section B of this chapter.

Questionnaire Construction

Unfortunately there are no established rules for constructing questionnaires. There are suggested guidelines and pitfalls to avoid, but questionnaire construction can only be learned by doing. However, some suggestions may be of use.

The first criterion for constructing any questionnaire is that the researcher developing the instrument be knowledgeable about the population being surveyed and have an understanding of the content area to be explored. Since it is usually not possible for one individual to be an expert in numerous areas, the task is best achieved when several persons work together.

Assuming that the researchers are armed with the necessary expertise, initial construction begins by outlining those content areas which most appropriately address the research question or questions.

For each content area, sub-topics are generated and all possible questions related to that topic are delineated. At this point, other questionnaires, known scales, and information from literature searches can be drawn together with the researcher's own listing of questions. The researcher is then ready to begin drafting the instrument. Reviewing other work is useful as an aid in the wording of items, to provide additional questions not previously considered, and to provide guidelines for the operationalization of concepts.

The instrument should begin and end with the least sensitive and emotionally charged items. In the beginning, the respondent must be engaged and not threatened by overly personal questions. The respondent's trust and interest must be gained so that he or she will feel comfortable enough to answer more personal and sensitive questions. In the same vein, the interview should not end with highly sensitive or emotional-provoking questions. That is not to say that questions which may cause some discomfort or be perceived as prying should all be grouped together, but rather that there should be an ebb and flow of questions that neither startles the respondent in the beginning nor leaves him or her upset at the end but does have some highs and lows in between.

Items should be simply worded and should ask one question only. For example, a question from the surveyed instruments in this report states: "Do you have difficulty falling asleep or waking up because you feel tense or depressed?" If the response is "yes," there are four possible situations that the respondent might mean: sleeplessness because of depression, sleeplessness because of tension, inability to wake-up because of depression, or inability to wake-up because of tension or a combination of both. Which of these, if any, is the researcher interested in? Assuming that one is seeking a specific data point, one way to approach this question, and other questions that need to be broken out, is to ask questions by component parts, such as the following:

1. Do you have difficulty getting to sleep at night?

    YES . . . . ASK A 1

    NO . . . . SKIP TO Q2 . . . 2

A. Why do you think you have difficulty getting to sleep? Would you say it is because of:

    Depression 1

    Tension 2

    or, some other cause (SPECIFY) _____

2. Do you have difficulty waking up once you've gotten to sleep?

    YES . . . . ASK A 1

    NO . . . . SKIP TO Q3 . . . 2

A. Why do you think you have difficulty waking up? Would you say it is because of:

    Depression 1

    Tension 2

    or, some other cause (SPECIFY)_____

This example illustrates a number of other key elements in questionnaire construction: 1. the use of closed-ended versus open-ended questions, 2. need for branching and use of skip patterns, 3. need for mutually exclusive categories, 4. consideration for the level of measurement, and 5. attention to precoding.

The example shows the use of closed-ended questions in the questions 1 and 2. This approach can be used to make the respondent give a precise answer, either yes or no. Additionally, it covers all of the possible responses. For instance, should the interviewee respond with don't know, no response, refuse to respond, or the question is not applicable, the interviewer may write-in what the circumstances were. That way, in coding and editing the data it is clear why that response may be missing, and it can be handled in the appropriate missing-data category during the analysis. Semi-opened questions such as in parts A or the sample questions where unanticipated responses are possible, responses can be specified so that these can also be handled in the editing process. The responses may generate several new categories, or they might be all classified together as "other."

To avoid compounding questions and to lead to other information, questionnaire designs should branch from the main question. Branching also clarifies the original question. When branching is used, the branches should be skipped if they are not applicable to the respondent based on his or her response to the original question. Since it is always more difficult for both the interviewer and the interviewee to move back through a questionnaire, when questions or portions of questions are skipped the skipping should always be in a forward direction.

Response categories should always be mutually exclusive. Just as problems are generated when too many questions are posed within one interview question, problems will arise if one response category is also part of another category. For example, this question was asked on one of the questionnaires surveyed:

Do you think the Hispanic elderly have difficulty receiving medical care because of:

1. Language barriers

2. Inability to communicate with the doctor

3. Cultural barriers

4. Lack of financial resources

5. Transportation

6. Other.

As can be seen, 1 and 2 are similar, and 3 might possibly be linked to 1 and 2. Likewise, lack of financial resources (4) may be the reason the respondent is unable to use transportation (5). Thus, the response categories overlap and will not provide the information sought from the question.

Both the previous example regarding depression and tension and this one on medical care are measured on nominal scales. Rather than enabling the researcher to use more rigorous multivariate parametric statistical techniques, they will result in more of a descriptive analysis. Thus the level of measurement will determine the level of analysis that can be used. The use of interval data usually means greater use of scales and indices in the survey instrument. This suggests that the researcher must have some sense of the level of statistical analysis that will be employed at the time the questionnaire is constructed or the questionnaire will dictate the type of analysis.

Precoding is closely related to this issue. To the extent possible, data should be coded and formatted on the questionnaire. This means that knowledge of the area is crucial. Data should be collected whenever possible at its highest level of measurement. This means continuous data should be collected rather than categorical data. For example, specific ages are better than age ranges, the exact number of years of schooling is preferable to general categories such as grammar school completion or high school completion. Data can always be collapsed, but once gathered in the categorical form it cannot be reversed. Finally, the data categories and precoding procedure should be developed with the analysis in mind.

In short, a questionnaire is not developed in a vacuum. The total research effort must be considered: the goals of the research, the specific information sought, the form in which the data will be retrieved, and the analysis to be employed.

The final step of questionnaire construction is pretesting of the instrument. All questionnaires should always be pretested. There is no short-cutting this step, for without pretesting the problems inherent in the questionnaire will never be detected until it is too late. The pretesting sample should be composed of respondents similar to those who will be the respondents in the main study. That way, in this step researchers will discover problems in wording, ambiguity, question flow, incomplete branching, skipping, time of interview administration, misunderstanding, and so forth. Problems of language translation will also emerge during this testing period. If substantial changes are made in the questionnaire as a result of the first pretest, a second or third pretest should be undertaken until the necessary changes are minimal.

Interviewers and Interviewing

Researchers have found that access to the elderly Hispanic and the probability of questionnaire completion is enhanced when interviewers and respondents share the same social class, ethnicity, sex, and age. The ideal interviewer for the Hispanic elderly is a bilingual older person who has lived in the community of the target population and is familiar with its culture and the lifestyles. In addition, the ideal interviewer would have an understanding of what is to be accomplished in a survey, and why the strict adherence to procedures is necessary. Usually few persons are available to fit this ideal role, thus it becomes necessary to train other older bilingual indigenous community members in the techniques of interviewing for surveys.

Bloom and Padilla (1979) identify potential areas of bias when indigenous interviewers are used. They found that respondents who perceive the interviewer as a peer will be tempted to answer in accordance with perceived peer group norms. Additionally, there is a problem maintaining scientific objectivity and neutrality. A peer interviewer may be more likely to score responses incorrectly because of an unconscious tendency to empathize with the problems and needs of the respondent. The result may be that the respondent's needs would be overemphasized while strengths would be underestimated.

On the other hand, two prevalent problems which can be minimized by using interviewers matched on these important characteristics with the interviewee are yea-saying and non-response.

Yea-saying is answering in agreement because the respondent feels that the answer is most appropriate and non-controversial. This problem usually occurs when the interviewer and respondent are different in terms of age, ethnicity, sex, or social class (Ragan and Cuellar, 1975). Even when interviewers are strictly matched with respondents in terms of ethnicity and age, yea-saying should be an expected phenomenon when the population under study is older, has a lower income, is of minority origin, and lacks more than six years of education. Ragan and Cuellar (1975) found significant effects attributable to yea-saying by older, lower social class Mexican Americans in Los Angeles. They attribute this, in part, to the difficulty of matching interviewers and respondents in terms of social class:

> The very requirements of the interviewer role (driver's license, automobile insurance, and a high degree of literacy and verbal skills) insure that interviewers will be of higher social status than a substantial number of respondents (Ragan and Cuellar, 1975).

Yea-saying can and should be addressed in research designs. Ragan and Cuellar (1975) identified some strategies which address the problem of yea-saying that tend to minimize it:

* avoid certain standard formats such as the agree-disagree format

* include contradictory items: opposite pairs operate both to counteract yea-saying tendencies and to provide a way to measure yea-saying

* reverse some items so that a favorable response requires a "disagree" answer and an unfavorable response requires an "agree" answer

* minimize the effect of social desirability by phrasing questions in such a way as to reduce social pressure

* arrange items to avoid biasing due to the order of presentation

* match the interviewer and interviewee as much as possible on ethnicity and sex

* have an idea of the response tendency of the group you are going to study when formulating the research design

* beware of applying scales that are developed on one population or subpopulation to another

* accept the inevitable bias, but estimate the severity of the problem

* report on response tendencies when reporting results of survey research. The research design should include a method for identifying response bias.

To minimize the problem of yea-saying in interviews, Bloom and Padilla (1979) add the following suggestions:

Select interviewers who are:

--- residents of the community to be studied

--- bilingual

--- interested in the research goals

--- equally divided among male and female in order to control for the effects of sex

--- paid a fee to sustain their motivation and reinforce the importance of their contribution

Finally, the panel of experts for this review of research instruments felt that the key to a successful interview was establishment of trust and rapport prior to the administration of the instrument. Without this atmosphere, the most perfectly matched interviewer will be unable to elicit quality responses. It was generally agreed that the ability to establish rapport required fluency in the respondent's language of preference, and a friendly, open attitude.

Interview refusals tend to be non-random, especially when the group studied is the elderly. Riley et al. (1972), for example, have shown that refusals tend to increase progressively by age, with incapacity and widowhood. Atchley (1969) found non-response is associated with persons who like to live alone and that social distance between the interviewer and respondent is associated with limited response and non-response.

Dowd and Ragan (1974), however, found high response rates among low-income Mexican-American elders in Los Angeles. They attributed this achievement to the following methodological procedures:

--- interviewers were matched on ethnicity and age (over 35 years old)

--- individually addressed letters were mailed to potential respondents explaining the study and informing them that they may be interviewed

--- respondents were made to feel that their opinions were important

--- persistent call-back procedures were used.

In summary, the Hispanic elderly are generally open and willing to submit to an interview if an appropriate effort is made. An appropriate effort would include selecting interviewers who are friendly, outgoing, and able to establish rapport with others. If, in addition, these interviewers are of the same ethnic group, sex, and speak the language of the respondent, then these characteristics will enhance the interview process. For the Hispanic elderly, in particular, the interviewer should be older, at least middle-aged. While it is not critical to the interview process, indigenous interviewers can be very helpful for bridging the gap to the community, and for providing insights into the community and easing the entry process.

D. TRANSLATION

In conducting research among elderly Hispanics it is imperative that there be a Spanish translation of the instrument. However, researchers should also be aware that the method of translation has significant implications for both validity and reliability. Most often researchers develop an English instrument and then translate it into Spanish. While this is a justifiable process, it is, nonetheless, necessary to verify equivalence. There are, obviously, serious problems that will be encountered if linguistic, conceptual, and contextual equivalence is not achieved. To aid researchers in their own translation tasks, this section discusses the translation process.

Equivalence

The process of developing equivalent-language versions of a survey instrument is not simply one of obtaining an accurate word-for-word translation of the original questionnaire; indeed, semantic equivalence is insufficient as a measure of equivalence of stimuli. Full equivalence is marked by the following characteristics: equivalent cultural meaning or conceptual equivalences, equivalent measurement or contextual equivalence, and finally, interwoven in those two, linguistic equivalence.

Equivalence of cultural meaning or what is termed conceptual equivalence is the assurance that the concepts being studied have any meaning or an equal meaning in the culture being studied. Concepts differ along many dimensions. There are those which are universal, such as "mother" or "illness", that transcend culture. However, there are concepts that have no direct equivalent in another language but have comparable definitions. For example, while there is no word for "mental illness" in Spanish that carries the same connotation as it does in English, there are comparable phrases which convey similar information. Thus the conceptual equivalence of the questions must be preserved even if it means adjusting exact linguistic equivalence.

57

Beyond the assurance of comparable conceptual meaning, the most difficult task is to assure equivalence of measurement, or, as we term it, contextual equivalence. That is, for the environment, are the concepts from both versions of the question measuring the same thing. If not there may be problems of validity. Unfortunately, this area receives the least attention yet is the source of most problems in Hispanic research. While most researchers can attend to the problems of linguistic and conceptual equivalence, few pay adequate attention to equivalence in measurement.

Finally, consideration should be given to regional differences in Spanish. For example, the word "bus" could be translated as "caminion", "guagua", or "autobus", depending on the dialect of the Spanish-speaking respondent. Misuse of regionally preferred words could result in respondent confusion, or nonresponse.

Approaches to Linguistic Equivalence

Questionnaire wording and translation are inseparable aspects of dual-language survey instruments. Given the difficulty in translating a poorly constructed questionnaire into another language, the following are useful guidelines in developing an original English language survey instrument (Brislin, et al., 1973; Lindholm et al., 1980).

1. Use short, simple sentences.

2. Employ the active rather than the passive voice.

3. Repeat nouns instead of using pronouns.

4. Avoid metaphors and colloquialisms. Such phrases are least likely to have an equivalent in the target language.

5. Avoid the subjective mode, for example, verb forms with "could" or "would".

6. Avoid adverbs and prepositions telling "where" or "when" (for example, frequent, beyond, upper).

7. Avoid possessive forms where possible.

8. Use specific rather than general terms (for example, name specific animals, such as cows, chickens, pigs, rather than using the general term "livestock").

9. Avoid words which indicate vagueness regarding some event or thing (for example, probably and frequently).

10. Avoid sentences with two different verbs if the verbs suggest different actions.

11. Utilize Latin root words rather than words which have Anglo-Saxon roots (for example, "systematic" rather than "planful").

Redundancy also amplifies the translation process. By including more than one question on the same concept, the translator gains additional material for measuring the area of interest. Redundancy also provides the researcher with the opportunity to conduct validity and reliability tests. An example of redundancy in a study of attitudes toward law enforcement might be: "Do the law enforcement agents work effectively in this town?"; and "How well do the policemen do their jobs?"

Decentering

The preceding suggestions increase the likelihood of developing a translatable English instrument, but they do not guarantee that all phrases or concepts will have an exact Spanish equivalent. Decentering can help insure the equivalence of stimuli items in both language versions of the final instrument.

Decentering refers to a translation process in which the original language version of the instrument and the target-language versions are equally important. With decentering, the initial-language version of the instrument is not the final version, but is subject to further amendments. This is mandatory for producing equivalent versions in two languages. Words and concepts that present translation problems are located by the back-translation process and omitted from the English version. Translating continues until the English version, now modified, is equivalent to the translated version. Equivalent items are then pretested to determine their meaning within the target population to insure measurement equivalence.

An item from a recently translated psychological test which contained untranslatable colloquialisms in its original English version exemplifies the decentering process (Lindholm, et al., 1980). When the item: "Do you believe that good guys come out second best?" was translated, the resultant Spanish version was: "cree usted que no vale la pena ser una buena persona?" Back translation of the Spanish version resulted in a contrasting version of the source item. Indeed, the Spanish translation is: "Do you believe that it's not worth the effort to be a nice person?" Hence, researchers should be cautious in their translation tasks.

59

Translation Techniques

The three most frequently used methods of translation are one-way translation, back-translation, and translation by committee.

One-way translation is the most common translation procedure. It is also the least-acceptable means of translating a survey research instrument. The procedure involves locating a qualified bilingual person and simply obtaining a translation of the original. The process does not employ decentering, and is likely to produce non-equivalent results, especially if the source version embodies colloquialisms or untranslatable words or concepts.

Back-translation was developed in response to the inherent weaknesses of one-way translation. In this method the instrument is translated from language A (source) to language B (target) by a native speaker of language B, then from B to A by a native speaker of A. The sequence is repeated until discrepancies in meaning are clarified or removed. By keeping the second (target to source) translator unaware of the original source-language version of the instrument, the researcher is provided with two versions of the source language from which words, phrases, or concepts which do not translate well can be identified. Discrepancies should be scrutinized to identify problems in the original source version, in the translation into the target language, or in the back-translation. By using decentering to eliminate problems in the original source version of the instrument, subsequent rounds of back-translation can be carried out until identical and appropriate pairs of source and target translations are derived.

Although the back-translation technique is acknowledged by researchers as the most reliable method of producing equivalent translations, it is not without problems. Theoretically, an equivalent translation of the original-language version should produce an identical back-translation. Brislin (1970) points out that back-translation may produce a spurious sense of equivalence because of the active role taken by bilingual translators. Translators may have a shared set of rules about translating specific nonequivalent words or phrases. Back-translators may not be able to clarify a poorly phrased target language version of a question. And finally, if the bilingual person translating the original source version to the target version retains unfamiliar grammatical forms of the source language, the person who back-translates may be unable to decifer these problems. A frequently encountered problem in this category is the retention of the passive voice in English while Spanish is primarily an active-voice language (Lindholm, et al., 1980).

Translation by committee involves a panel of bilingual persons who translate from source to target language, then convene to compare results. Although this method is less cumbersome than the process

60

of back-translation, it is subject to several possible sources of error (Werner and Campbell, 1970). The major problem involved is the possibility of shared misconceptions by the committee as a result of social class or differential linguistic experiences (for example, a member of a Hispanic subgroup translating for another subgroup). Translators might also hedge on criticizing a colleague. The limitations of the committee approach to translations suggest that it is best as an adjunct to more reliable translation procedures such as back-translation (Brislin, et al., 1973).

Pretest Techniques

All questionnaires require pretesting. Consequently, researchers have developed a number of techniques for evaluating the accuracy and relevance of translated items. These techniques, using bilingual people or a panel of experts, do not constitute an acceptable alternative to a field pretest. Rather, they should be seen as possible adjuncts to field pretesting.

A committee of experts, although inadequate as a primary means of translation, can be useful as an adjunct to back-translation for identifying translation problems that have slipped through the decentering process. For example, a panel of bilinguals can be used to examine the target version without knowledge of the source version. Lindholm, et al., (1980) suggest the use of this procedure as a means of adapting questionnaires to comply with regionally preferred language usage. They suggest that the final target-language questionnaire include, for example, Mexican, Puerto Rican, and Cuban variants of a word in order to insure respondent comprehension.

Bilingual Pretesting is another procedure for testing the accuracy of source and target versions of an instrument. Both the target and source versions are administered to bilinguals. The researcher then looks for response differences, either by observation or through statistical tests, in each item when administered to the same individual in different languages. The validity of this method of testing for linguistic equivalence is questionable because bilinguals may not always produce similar responses to the same item in two languages. Indeed, language, which is a function of cultural context in which it is learned and used, may vary between bilingual persons.

Field Pretesting is indispensable even after the most carefully controlled translation procedure. Field testing techniques require that the questionnaire be administered to typical representatives of the target population. After the participant responds to the item, or to a probing question about the item, the interviewer asks: "What do you mean?" If the justification for the response is incongruous with what the interviewer expects, it is assumed that the intended meaning of the item is not being conveyed. This technique can be useful in identifying questions that test for conceptual equivalence. Another field pretest technique is to ask the respondent: "What do you think this question means?" in reference to the survey-instrument items, or ask the respondent to paraphrase the item. This procedure allows the researcher to ascertain whether the connotative intent of the question has been transferred to the target language. Field testing gives researchers the opportunity to identify measurement problems and it provides a reliability and validity check on the applicability of the measurements.

In summary, the following suggestions concerning equivalence issues have been suggested (Warwick and Osherson, 1973).

1. Linguistic equivalence is inseparable from research concept and design. The choice of a research problem salient to both of the cultures involved is one of the most effective aids to linguistic equivalence.

2. Many problems of translation can be avoided by advance familiarity with the cultures being studied.

3. The primary emphasis in translation should be on conceptual equivalence (comparability of ideas) rather than formally identical words (semantic equivalence) in each culture.

4. Back-translation and decentering are valuable tools in the development of linguistically equivalent source and target language versions of a survey instrument.

5. Independent of the use of back-translation and decentering, conceptual-contextual-linguistic equivalence can be improved through the extensive pretesting of the research instruments in the target culture.

E. RELIABILITY AND VALIDITY

Social research is concerned, for the most part, with explaining or increasing one's understanding about some social phenomena. Theory is most often the guiding light in this venture. Theory explains and enhances our understanding of some specific problem area. However, unless theory can be put to the test, our knowledge in problem areas will not be extended. In this light, measurement is the link between theory and research. Measurement is the process by which one operationalizes concepts to be used in the research endeavor. If, however, theory is to be meaningful and the piece of research relevant, measures used in the investigation must be adequate indicants of the concepts being used. In addition, these concepts should generate the same or nearly the same findings over repeated administrations. If measurement fails to accomplish this end, the initial aim of the research task has been abrogated.

Of course, these comments about the utility of empirical referents forms the core issues of the validity/reliability dilemma. The present section has three objectives: 1) to elaborate on the topic of reliability/validity; 2) to discuss problems one faces by not having reliable and valid measures; and 3) to illustrate how validity and reliability problems are exacerbated in cross-cultural research.

Validity

Validity is concerned with efficacy: the degree to which an item measures what it purports to measure. However, validity is never fully achieved, it is a matter of degree. There are three types of validity: face validity, criterion validity, and construct validity.

1. Face Validity

Face validity, sometimes called content validity, is the easiest validation procedure to use but the most difficult to carry out. Face validity is a matter of judgment. The judgment is based on whether the question or item captures the definition of the concept measured, and whether that information being gathered is germane to the concept. Face validity is simply assessed by the evaluator studying the concept to be measured and determining through his judgment whether the instrument arrives at the concept adequately. It should be kept in mind however, that arriving at face validity is not an easy task because the more complex the concept, the more difficult it is to arrive at some agreed upon universe of content. These are some weaknesses characterizing content validity. First, one must accept the universe of content as defining the variable of interest. Second, there is no agreed upon criterion for determining the extent to which a measure has achieved face validity.

2. Criterion Validity

Criterion validity, also called concurrent validity or predictive validity, involves multiple measurement of the same concept. The process entails use of a second measure of a concept as the criterion against which the new measure may be checked.

There are, however, a number of weaknesses characterizing criterion validity. To begin with, the correlation between a measurement instrument and some criterion is the only data we have in making a decision about an instrument's validity. And, as Nunnally (1967) writes, "...if it were found that accuracy in horseshoe pitching correlated highly with success in college, horseshoe pitching would be a valid measure for predicting success in college." Thus, criterion validity lends itself to be used atheoretically. Second, and this may be the case especially in the social sciences, there may not be any criterion available with which we can assess the validity of a measurement instrument. For example, what would be an appropriate criterion for life satisfaction?

3. Construct Validity

Construct validity concerns the relationships among concepts and the measurement instrument which have been specified within a theoretical framework as a set of testable hypotheses. For example, suppose an acculturation scale was begin used among elderly Hispanics and predicted that persons rating high on acculturation (the degree to which individuals take on the cultural traits of another group) might participate in activities most often associated with citizenship, such as voting, espousing certain values, etc. If the correlation between acculturation and some form of behavior or attitudes is both positive and significant, we then have one piece of information supporting the construct validity of the acculturation scale.

There are three steps one should follow in arriving at construct validity (but such validity, like the other two, is never fully assured). First, one should specify the relationship between the concepts of interest. Second, one examines these relationships. And, finally, the findings should be interpreted in light of how they clarify the construct validity of the measurement instrument. The important point, however, is that theory guides construct validity. It is not imperative that one formulate a large and fully developed complex formal theory, but rather, that one state theoretically derived hypotheses regarding the relationships among the concepts of interest.

Reliability

Reliability refers to consistency: the degree to which an item derives the same findings over repeated administrations or different samples. For example, we would expect a value orientation scale (Szapocznik et al., 1978) to derive the same information if administered to the same population over a period of time, or among different populations. As is the case with validity, reliability is also never fully achieved; it too is a matter of degree. Four methods for measuring reliability--the retest method, the alternative-form method, the split halves method, and the internal consistency method--will be discussed here.

1. The Retest Method

In the retest method, the same instrument is given to the same

groups of persons after a certain period of time has elapsed. Correla1
are then computed between the scores on the two tests. The assum
is that the computed correlation will be substantial because both sc
are measuring the same thing.

While retest procedures are appealing, they are, nonethe
characterized by some important limitations. Researchers, for
most part, gather data at one point in time because gathering
at two or more points in time can be expensive. In addition,
correlations in the retest may indicate that the underlying co
may have elicited a difference because of changes in events occu
in the elapsed time interval. For example, using the acculturation s
if the scores on this instrument do not correlate positively when i
been administered at two points in time, it may reflect a chan
acculturation of the sample. While new arrivals to this country
initially acculturate quickly, a number of phenomena, ranging
discrimination to disappointment with the society's opportunity stru
may enhance their own ethnic/racial identity.

A second problem concerns "reactivity". Reactivity refers
individual's increased sensitivity to some phenomenon. In the p
of measuring a person at time one on some measure of cultural awar
for instance, may change his awareness, and this may be reflec
the retest correlation.

A final problem concerns memory. Correlation may be in
because taking a test at time one increases one's familiarity wi
test, and therefore, influences responses at time two. Obvious
memory effect depends on the time interval between test one an
two. The shorter the time interval, the greater the memory e
and the greater the correlation.

2. Alternative-Form Method

The alternative form method is similar to the retest meth
difference is that rather than administering the same test at ti
and time two, one administers an alternative form of the test a
two. The correlations between the two tests is the estimate of reli

While this procedure is superior to the retest method, b
it reduces memory effects, there are certain weaknesses ass
with it. It does not distinguish true change from unreliability.
it is suggested that topics be chosen which are not subject to chang

A second problem with this procedure is the difficulty one
have in finding alternative or parallel forms of the same test. By
tests is meant tests that have the same true scores and equal varia

65

3. Split-Halves Method

The split halves method can be done in one testing and entails dividing the total set of items into halves. The scores on the halves are then correlated in deriving a coefficient of reliability.

The major problem with using the split halves method concerns its arbitrariness: the odd numbers are placed in one half, and the even in another. However, there are other ways one may go about splitting up the items and there is some indication that correlations differ depending on which procedure is used.

4. Internal Consistency Method

Two measures of internal consistency are Cronbach's alpha and the Kuder Richardson coefficient. Neither procedure requires that the items be split or repeated at two points in time. Cronbach's alpha is:

$$= N/ \left\{ (N-1) \left[1 - \Sigma \rho^2 (Y_i) \right] / \rho_x^2 \right.$$

where N is the number of items; $\Sigma \rho^2 (Y_i)$ is equal to the sum of the item variances; and ρ_x^2 is equal to the variance of the total composite. If one is using correlations rather than variances the following is appropriate:

$$N\bar{p} / (1 + \bar{p} (N-1))$$

where N is the number of items and $\bar{p}$ is equal to the mean interitem correlation. The coefficient depends on the average interitem correlation and number of items in the scale. As the average interitem correlation among the items increases, and as the number of items increase, alpha increases. The interpretation of alpha lies in the expected correlation between the test and a hypothetical alternative form of the same length--which may never be constructed.

Alpha has the following limitations: first, adding items reduces the reliability. Second, the more items in an instrument, the more time and resources are spent in its construction. Third, alpha is more difficult to compute than other forms of reliability, although it has the same logical status as coefficients from the other methods.

Cronbach's alpha is an extension of an estimate computed by Kuder and Richardson (1937). The major difference is that the Kuder-Richardson coefficient is based on items which are dichotomously coded. The Kuder-Richardson coefficient is:

$$KR20 = N/(N-1)\ (1 - p_i q_i/\beta_x^2)$$

where N is the number of dichotomous items; p_i is the proportion responding "positively" to the ith item; q_i is equal to $1 - p_i$ and is the variance of the total composite. KR20 is subject to the same limitations as Cronbach's alpha.

The Consequences of Invalid and Unreliable Measures

If one does not have valid measures, something else is being measured and subsequently leads to misleading findings. While the use of invalid measures may make the investigation unusable, unreliable measures have different consequences such as the inability to generalize beyond the data, biased results, and limited outcomes relevant to specific cultural concerns.

The ability to generalize beyond one's data is a primary objective of both theory and research. Social scientists are continually attempting to expand the use of their concepts to other samples and populations in their quest for a universal understanding of social behavior. Obviously, if an item(s) is not consistent, its generalizability is drastically curtailed. The concept then generates different results when administered to different samples. In any event, the desired effect, generalizability, is lost.

A second dilemma encountered when using unreliable measures is that they may be biased. Assuming that an item is valid, bias may be introduced because its validity is sample specific, that is, characteristic of a specific sample. When sample specific instruments are administered to different samples, one encounters results which are not theoretically accurate.

The interview setting can greatly hinder reliability. Three dilemmas arise from the interview setting. First, the presence of third persons biases responses because third persons influence an interviewee's responses. Indeed, it is not uncommon for a third person to answer all questions for a respondent. Second, community attitudes affect responses, that is, interviewees may answer what they perceive to be appropriate responses, i.e., normative answers. Third, fear of reprisal will hinder reliability, or cause unwillingness to answer certain questions.

Finally, a lack of cultural familiarity by researchers with the culture of interest will hinder reliability. Lack of familiarity with a specific culture can, for instance, cause problems with sensitive questions, such as questions pertaining to politics or sexual behavior. On the other hand, not knowing that certain concepts do not have an equivalent concept will also cause reliability dilemmas. Often asking questions of women, rather than men, will contribute problems in male dominant cultures.

In the field of Social Gerontology, research has relied on the validity and reliability of instruments standardized on white middle-class respondents which fail to consider the unique cultural characteristics and attitudes of Hispanic elderly (Montiel, 1975). The solution to such problems has been to reconstruct instruments and methods to insure the absence of such cultural skewness (Moore, 1971; Cuellar, 1974; Montiel, 1975; Manuel and Bengtson, 1976).

Theoretically, it can be expected that an English language interview instrument may be worded only slightly different for a sample group if the only difference is, for example, social class. However, in cases when an English language instrument, standardized on an Anglo sample, is applied to a low-income and ethnic minority where English is a second language, new variables are introduced which may then lead to major conceptual problems (Peterson, Mangen, and Sanders, 1978). Reconstructing the methodology and instrument would enhance reliability and validity.

Familiarity with the Hispanic community can lead to many advantages (Sotomayor, 1975; Cuellar, 1978; Montero, 1977; Torres-Gil, 1976; Trimble, 1977; Myers, 1974). For example, cultural sanction might eliminate the bias introduced by normative responses and/or fear or reprisal from governmental agencies. Bengtson and Ragan (1977) point out that among Mexican-Americans "fear and resentment engendered by perceived recent 'sweeps' by government officials to identify and deport illegal aliens, would have contributed to a respondent's lack of cooperation and negated reliability." However, because the authors were able to receive legitimization from the community, these problems were, to a great degree, resolved. In addition, because of cultural familiarity introduced by the utilization of a community panel on the research staff, the term "Chicano" (an offensive term to many elderly Mexican-Americans) was dropped from the instrument (see, also, Valle and Mendoza (1978) for a related issue).

Salience of instruments and concepts is also enhanced by reconstructing the methods and the questionnaire. For example, a considerable body of research points out that minority elderly suffer "double jeopardy", i.e., disadvantages associated with minority status and those related to aged status (Dowd and Bengtson, 1978; U.S. Senate Special Committee on Aging, 1971). If this argument is true, then researchers must be skeptical about the reliability and validity of any measure applied to minority elderly, since it is designed to account only for aging related (singular) problems.

In sum, numerous methodological problems exist with respect to conducting research among elderly Hispanics, problems which have strong implications for both reliability and validity of research instruments, and therefore, the important consequences for one's findings.

The lack of rigor in the construction of instruments "...drastically impairs the comparability of measures within a domain and weakens the cumulative impact of multiple researchers" (Peterson et al., 1978).

CHAPTER III

NARRATIVE ABSTRACTS OF INSTRUMENTS

Through a variety of processes outlined in the Appendix, questionnaires used to evaluate some facet of the Hispanic elderly population were selected and reviewed by a panel of researchers and a panel of community elderly residing in East Los Angeles. While other research instruments have been used in surveys which incorporated some Hispanic elderly in the overall sample, this specific subgroup was consistently omitted from analysis. In general, this bias occurred because the investigators who designed these instruments did not perceive their work as either elderly-or Hispanic-related.

The narrative abstracts of this chapter provide an overview of the research for which these instruments were the primary data-gathering tools. Additionally, the narratives briefly discuss the instruments' specific applicability to Hispanic elders. These brief discussions are drawn from the general comments provided by the expert panel and the community panel noted above.

Each instrument has been assigned a four digit code. The four digit numbers were assigned according to the following system.

The first number identifies the group that is the focus of research; the second identifies the content area addressed; the third identifies the languages in which the instrument is available; and, the fourth identifies the number in the series of instruments based on the preceding coding criteria of one, two, and three, the group, content area, and language of the instrument.

Therefore, the codes read as follows:

First Digit: Target Group, Focus of the Research

0   Hispanic Elderly
1   All Elderly (includes Hispanics in the sample)
2   All Ages (includes Hispanic elderly in sample)

Second Digit: Content Area

0   Needs Assessment (covers a variety of topics for program planning)

1   Mental Health/Physical Health (focuses investigation on this specific topic)

2   Social Service Utilization (surveys use of social services in general)

3   Employment/Retirement

4   Cultural Values/Norms (assesses perceptions of aging, family interaction, and ascertains the value base of the culture)

5   Acculturation (focuses on measuring acculturation)

6   Social Support/Networks

7   Leisure/Recreation

8   General (covers a variety of topics for baseline information but not specifically as a needs assessment)

9   Other

Third Digit: Language Availability

0   Available in English and Spanish
1   Available in English only
2   Available in Spanish only

Fourth Digit: Number in the Series

The number in the series that have the same first three digits.

For example, 0001 means that the instrument focuses on Hispanic elderly, is a needs assessment, is available in both English and Spanish, and is distinguished from other Hispanic elderly needs assessments by the fourth digit.

This numbering system allows the reader to add his or her own critiques of still other instruments and to maintain a systematic file. The narratives represent the current state-of-the-art. As such, they should prove useful to the reader or researcher for further studies on Hispanic elders in the U.S.

NEEDS ASSESSMENT QUESTIONNAIRE

Description:

This is a national survey of the needs of the Hispanic elderly. It includes such items as transportation, employment, housing, neighborhood, health, mental health, income, nutrition, social services, activities, discrimination, media and finally a section on problems of older Hispanics.

The interview length is about 1½ hours. It was administered face-to-face by project-trained interviewers who were bicultural and bilingual.

The instrument is constructed of closed-ended and multiple-choice items, and is a composite of other instruments. It includes scales addressing life satisfaction and social contact.

The instrument information was originally designed in English and later translated into Spanish.

Although information on reliability and validity is unavailable, the panel of experts judged this instrument as moderate to good in those categories.

Use with Hispanic Elderly

Technically this instrument is well done. The categories are easy to follow, wording is direct, instructions are clear, and it is well laid out. It is appropriate for elderly of different age levels, and content areas are relevant; however, it is somewhat long and requires a good attention span.

The instrument is middle-class oriented and does not account for life experiences such as poverty and its residuals during old age. There is a certain lack of sensitivity in dealing with family problems which may offend the pride of some elderly. Specific problems of minority groups are not addressed, nor are ethnic preferences.

Linguistically, the instrument tends to favor the Mexican-American who has attained written and verbal fluency in Spanish.

For further information, contact:

Carmela Lacayo
Asociacion Nacional Pro-Personas Mayores
1730 W. Olympic Blvd., Suite 401
Los Angeles, CA 90015
Telephone: (213) 487-1922

RURAL AGING SURVEY

Description:

This questionnaire is concerned with defining the characteristics of the Spanish-speaking elderly with a migrant or seasonal farmwork background. It surveys needs in health, nutrition, housing, income, employment, and transportation. Communication skills are assessed and particular attention is paid to the use of services, and to rural problems arising as the result of a migrant pattern.

This instrument was used in two separate studies:

1) Mexican-American Elderly of Idaho, particularly rural agricultural workers; administered by the Idaho Migrant Council.

2) Aged-Anglo and Hispanic Seasonal Migrant Workers for the California Migrant and Seasonal Farmworkers Council.

In California, the sampling design specified a proportional random sampling in 10 migrant camps, in rural counties, and in East Los Angeles. The sample was stratified according to census estimates of a county's percentage of Spanish-speaking families. The interviewers were bicultural, bilingual representatives recruited from local migrant farmworkers' social service agencies.

In Idaho, the sample included low-income, minority, limited English-speaking individuals, and the rural elderly.

The instrument is constructed with both open and closed-ended questions, and it contains one Likert-type scale on daily and social needs. The face-to-face interview can be conducted in approximately 45 minutes.

The instrument is available in English and in a Spanish version geared to the Mexican-American idiom. The instrument was translated from English to Spanish. Both versions were pretested. Reliability was determined through internal consistency and test-retest with face validity.

Use with Hispanic Elderly:

This questionnaire is relatively short and well-formatted. The questions are explicit and the instructions are adequately presented. The Spanish version from California uses a colloquial idiom appropriate to age and culture; however, there are problems with linguistic

74

equivalence which will cause data-analysis problems.

There is no Spanish version for the Idaho study. Presumably the English was translated during the time of the interview by a bilingual interviewer. This instrument could be summarized as a brief needs assessment, specifically geared to the older farmworker (50+). Items and issues, however, are not specific to the Hispanic.

The instrument may be obtained without expense from:

1) Roger Granado, Executive Director
   La Cooperativa Campesian de California
   1010 J Street, Suite A
   Sacramento, CA 95814
   Telephone: (916) 322-1283

2) Lydia Goodhue, Acting Director
   Aging Project
   715 So. Capitol Blvd., Suite 405
   Boise, Idaho 83706
   Telephone: (208) 345-9761

MEXICAN AMERICAN ELDERLY IN THREE
COLORADO COMMUNITIES

Description:

This instrument is a needs assessment of older Mexican Americans living in three communities in Colorado (urban, small town, and rural). The areas of inquiry include household composition, transportation, use of time, finances, savings, program utilization, family networks, informal supports, health and medications, dental care, activities of daily living, attitudes toward living arrangements, and education.

This is a short interview schedule consisting of 81 open and closed items. It was administered in a face-to-face interview of about 30 minutes by project-trained interviewers who were bilingual and bicultural. The Spanish version is a direct translation of the English, validated through back-translation by an external translator.

No formal tests of reliability and validity were performed; however, the instrument was pretested for comprehension.

Use with Hispanic Elderly:

Very few items in this survey are directed toward the cultural experience of the Hispanic, and no areas are examined in depth. The response choices are inadequate and items lack space for comments. The Spanish-language translation is a good one, but it does not make this instrument more relevant to Spanish speakers. This brief interview could be used as a source for items, or as the base for developing a more in-depth instrument.

There is no cost for this instrument; however, permission to replicate is required. Please contact:

Miriam Orleans, Ph.D.
Department of Preventive Medicine
P.O. Box C-245
University of Colorado
Denver, CO 80262

SAN MATEO'S SPANISH SPEAKING SENIOR CITIZENS
PROJECT QUESTIONNAIRE

Description:

This instrument is a needs assessment of the Spanish-speaking elderly of Northern San Mateo County, California. Questions are asked in the areas of demographic, health and dental needs, in-home support services, housing, nutrition program use, transportation, legal services, employment, finances, information and referral services, and mental health services.

The questionnaire is an original construction which is short and employs predominately closed-ended questions. The interviews were conducted by monolingual Spanish-speaking community workers who were also senior citizens trained to administer the interview in a face-to-face session. The interview time is between 20 and 30 minutes.

The instrument was developed to gather information for a model social-service delivery system for Spanish-speaking seniors, and it was used by various agencies to improve their social-service programs. The research population included the bilingual elderly of Daly City and San Francisco who were referred to the project by senior groups and agencies, by a friend, or by self. Because of the nature of the demonstration project, reliability and validity studies were not done.

Use with Hispanic Elderly:

This questionnaire is intended to specifically identify needs of the Hispanic elderly. The language is simple, clear and appropriate for the age cohort. The instrument focuses on reasons for non-use of services. It reflects sound knowledge of the target population, for example, the respondent might not use transportation because of fear which is an important unexplored issue. This concept can be extended to other areas of technical innovation such as the telephone and elevators. The question of being embarrassed by dental problems was raised, and such questions may extend to other health problems, legal help, and so forth. The questionnaire does not cover cultural issues comprehensively, and lacks items on family and family-support systems; however, as a brief needs assessment it does a very adequate job.

It may be obtained at no cost from:

Shea Muller
San Mateo Area Agency on Aging
617 Hamilton
Redwood City, CA 94063
Telephone: (415) 364-5600, Ext. 4511

l Stop.

SURVEY OF NEEDS AND RESOURCES AMONG
AGED MEXICAN-AMERICANS

Description:

This assessment of the needs of elderly Mexican Americans was prepared for the Texas Governor's Committee on Aging. Categories of inquiry include religion, immigration, perceptions of old age, problems of the elderly, local and government agencies as resources, family and church as resources, and ethnicity.

The interview consists of 26 open and closed-ended items in Spanish which are administered by a bicultural/bilingual interviewer in approximately 25 minutes.

No information on the target population or reliability and validity studies is available.

Use with Hispanic Elderly:

This survey is very culture specific, and includes most issues faced by the Hispanic elderly. The language is simple, direct, and appropriate for the targeted elderly. This is a survey which could be expanded and used in further research.

The instrument can be obtained from:

Texas Technical University
Lubbock, TX 79409

ASSESSMENT OF THE MENTAL HEALTH STATUS, REHABILITATION NEEDS AND BARRIERS TO HEALTH UTILIZATION AMONG OLDER HISPANIC IN LOS ANGELES COUNTY

Description:

The purpose of this current project is to gather information on the health-care problems and needs of the older Hispanic population of Los Angeles County. The focus of the data gathering is on the most serious mental health and health problems, physical symptoms, rehabilitation needs, and functional problems affecting older Hispanics. The study will rely on self-report and objective information regarding specific symptoms, attitudes, and expectations about health care, patterns of utilization, access barriers, and knowledge of current health problems.

One thousand elderly--60 years of age and over--who identify their national heritage with a Spanish-speaking country will be included in the study. This group will include first, second, and third generation Hispanics who reside in Los Angeles County. The sampling procedure is a multi-stage, area-probability selection with demographic and geographic stratification introduced in each stage.

The instrument to be used is the Comprehensive Assessment and Referral Evaluation (CARE) developed by Gurland et al. (1977). The CARE is a multidisciplinary, personal-interview guide which covers psychiatric, medical, functional, nutritional, economic and social problems. The respondent's self-reported data and behavior, as observed by the interviewer, are used by the latter to write narrative summaries and to reach a global judgment about the respondent's condition.

The instrument has been subjected to validity and reliability testing. (See: Barry Gurland et al. "The Comprehensive Assessment and Referral Evaluation (CARE)--Rationale, Development, and Reliability" International Journal of Aging and Human Development, Vol. 8 (1), 1977, p. 9-42.) Additionally, the CARE has evolved from the Present State Examination (PSE) and the Mental Health Status Schedule (MSS). (See: R.L. Spitzer et al. "The Mental Status Schedule: Rationale, Reliability and Validity" Comprehensive Psychiatry, Vol. 5, 1964, p. 384-395, and J.K. Wing et al. "Reliability of a Procedure for Measuring Present Psychiatric State" British Journal of Psychiatry, Vol. 113, 1967, p. 449-515.)

The instrument has been translated into Spanish and was back-translated by a panel of Hispanic researchers. The language was found to be equivalent and appropriate for the target population. Administration time is approximately two hours.

Use with Hispanic Elderly:

This instrument is useful as an evaluation tool for placement if it is administered by health and mental health professionals. It has not been previously used with Hispanics as the target population. Its value as a survey instrument administered by persons not trained in the health and mental health field who are bicultural and bilingual is highly questionable. It is lengthy and leaves responses to questions to the interviewer's judgment.

This instrument has been copyrighted and requires permission of the authors to use. For further information on this instrument and this project contact:

Waldo Lopez
Rancho Los Amigos Hospital
Adult Senior Center
7601 East Imperial Highway
Downey, CA 90242
Telephone: (213) 922-7403

COPING MECHANISMS AND UTILIZATION
OF COMMUNITY SERVICES

Description:

This instrument was designed to investigate the utilization patterns of health and welfare services among the Spanish-speaking elderly in East Los Angeles, to explore coping mechanisms, to assess attitudes towards the aging process, and finally to explore differences between males and females in these areas of concern.

It covers the following categories of items: physical health, mental health, subjective perceptions of health, community interaction, problems of aging, and past and present employment patterns.

This originally designed instrument contains 81 closed-ended questions and includes four Likert scales: the Health Opinion Survey, Srole's Anomia Scale, Ragan's Health Scale and the Life Satisfaction Index of Neugarten, Harughuist and Tobin, which measure stress anomie, functional abilities, and life satisfaction, respectively.

The face-to-face interviews were conducted in Spanish or English, according to preference. Interview time averaged one and one-half hours. Interviewers were social work students. The research population consisted of 100 Hispanic seniors drawn from a health-screening program.

Use with Hispanic Elderly:

The research focused on Mexican-American elderly and issues specific to this group. The Spanish translation was appropriate for this target group. The scales, however, were developed for a target population of the dominant Anglo culture and appear to be inappropriate for measurement of Hispanics and for the content and design of the instrument since they reduce its flow and continuity. A major problem with this instrument is that it was designed to gather information on so many diverse areas. The result is that sections lack depth and contain only one or two items.

This is a short and simple instrument and it could be used as a resource for development of other questionnaires on the Hispanic elderly.

This instrument has been copyrighted by the author, but can be obtained at no cost from:

Dr. Ramon Salcido
University of Southern California
School of Social Work
University Park
Los Angeles, CA 90007
Telephone: (213) 634-7815

A NEEDS ASSESSMENT OF OLDER HISPANICS
IN OMAHA

Description:

This is a needs assessment of older Hispanics residing in Omaha, Nebraska, to determine the degree to which Omaha Hispanics are aware of and participate in available services for the elderly and the factors contributing to the use and non-use of those services. Areas covered include leisure time, ethnicity, service utilization, housing, employment and education.

The instrument is an original construction which contains 73 closed-ended questions. The interviewers were project trained bilingual Hispanics in their mid-years who administered the interview in a 40 minute face-to-face session. Respondents were encouraged to select the most comfortable language for conversing.

The identification of potential respondents was accomplished through contact with agencies, churches, and older Hispanics. The study groups consisted of 80 Mexican, Cuban and other Latino elderly.

The final instrument was translated into vernacular Spanish by two bilingual Omaha Hispanics, and was tested for reliability and validity.

Use with Hispanic Elderly:

This instrument is well focused for use with Hispanics since it asks for specific cultural references, such as Spanish-speaking services and programs, and contains many items on discrimination, transportation, and medical care for Hispanics. Items are sensitive to the elderly but do not include the rural population. The Spanish-language translation has many spelling errors; however, the vocabulary is appropriate for use with all Hispanic sub-groups.

Generally this instrument is well formatted, not too long, areas covered seem sufficient, and instructions to interviewers very sound. It functions well as a needs assessment.

Although use of this instrument requires the author's permission, it can be obtained at no cost from:

Dr. David R. Di Martino, Senior Research Associate
Center for Applied Urban Research
University of Nebraska-Omaha
PKCC, 1313 Farnam-on-the-Mall
Omaha, NE 68182
Telephone: (402) 554-3401

PROJECTO INDEPENDENCIA

Description:

The purpose of this survey was to test obstacles to service delivery based on the aging process and cultural variables, and to assess the degree of contact with informal support systems: family, church, and community organizations. The areas of inquiry cover transportation, health, program participation, barriers to utilization, neighborhood safety, informal help networks, and discrimination according to age and culture.

This is an original instrument consisting of open and closed-ended questions in English which are to be asked in a face-to-face interview by a Spanish speaking interviewer in English. Interviewers were project-trained indigenous workers. They administered the interview in approximately 45 minutes. It was subjected to test-retest for reliability.

Use with Hispanic Elderly:

This survey is specifically concerned with issues pertinent to Hispanic elders, and it probably will elicit much information on: discrimination, availability of Spanish language services, helping networks, education, health, and transportation. The lack of a Spanish language translation, however, could be problematic for researchers.

To use the instrument you must obtain the author's permission; however, the instrument can be obtained at no cost from:

Pamela Marques
847 Fox
Denver, CO 80204
Telephone: (303) 825-6841

HISPANIC ELDERLY EMPLOYMENT QUESTIONNAIRE

Description:

This is a survey of the work history of the elderly Hispanic living in the Boston area. It includes items in the following categories: employment history, training, migration, health, work satisfaction, discrimination, social origins and demographics, education, housing, community satisfaction, service utilization, social isolation, and acculturation.

The instrument is primarily an original construction; however, items from other instruments are included. It is composed of 105 items which are a combination of open and closed-response and multiple-choice questions. It also includes Likert scales.

The instrument is available in English and in a Spanish version which has been verified by back-translation. The interview was administered in one-hour sessions by indigenous interviewers who were matched on ethnicity and socioeconomic status. The Spanish version was subjected to tests of reliability and validity. The targeted population were all Hispanic workers, predominately Puerto Rican, age 55 and over, who resided in the area of Boston, Massachusetts.

Use with Hispanic Elderly:

This is an unusually good survey of the history and conditions of the elder Hispanic worker. Specific cultural issues such as discrimination, language use, and availability of training are covered in depth. The Spanish translation is very good, although the level of language used is rather formal for the targeted population. Many items apply only to Boston; however, most of this instrument can be used universally. It is an excellent model and source for items.

The author's permission is required to replicate this instrument. It can be obtained from:

Ana Maria Perez, M.S.W.
Hispanic Office of Planning
  and Evaluation, Inc.
628 Tremont Street
Boston, MA 92118
Telephone: (617) 424-1394

RETIREMENT: A DIFFERENTIAL EXPERIENCE FOR MEXICAN-AMERICANS AND ANGLOS

Description:

This survey was undertaken to broaden the understanding of today's national retirement policy (Social Security) as it relates to the life-experience perceptions of retired male Mexican Americans and Anglos. Specific categories covered are: understanding of retirement policy, worklife and retirement patterns, income, satisfaction in retirement, and perceptions of the retirement experience.

This is an original construction consisting of 60 open and closed-ended questions, including one Likert-type scale. The instrument is available in English and Spanish, and is administered face-to-face in less than one hour.

The study population included 72 male retired Mexican Americans and Anglos aged 55 and over. They were selected from Senior Center programs in Santa Fe, New Mexico, and Phoenix, Arizona.

Items were tested for reliability and validity using Spearman's Split-Half Technique and Pearson's Product Moment Correlation. The results indicated a high degree of correlation. The instrument was also subjected to peer review and judged reliable and valid.

Use with Hispanic Elderly:

This is a short instrument which has a good focus on the specific content area; however, culture-specific issues are lacking. A major problem is the phrasing of the questions which makes it sound like a school examination and therefore, somewhat intimidating. Females in retirement were excluded; however, the instrument is a good source for items and a model for more in-depth research in the area.

The schedule can be obtained for a fee from:

University Microfilms International
300 North Zeeb Road
Ann Arbor, Michigan 48106

or

Margaret Dieppa
P.O. Box 26408
Tempe, AZ 85282
Telephone: (602) 261-5931

A STUDY OF CHICANO GRANDPARENTS IN DENVER

Description:

This is an investigation of coping patterns, cultural practices, and structural arrangements and beliefs among aged Chicano grandparents. The research explored the function of the grandparents in relation to: (a) child rearing, (b) family crises, (c) authority and decision-making in the family, (d) the teaching of religion, (e) the transmission of history, folklore, language and custom.

The instrument is an original construction consisting of 64 open and closed-ended items. It was administered by project-trained indigenous interviewers who were also professionals in social research. They were matched to respondents on ethnicity and language. The survey was given as an "on the spot" translation of the English and averaged about 45 minutes.

The target population was 38 individuals in 30 households located in the Denver barrio, and all were Chicano grandparents aged 55 to 91 years of age. No studies of reliability and validity were reported, although the instrument was pretested. Five propositions for research were generated from this survey, and it resulted in the author's doctoral dissertation.

Use with Hispanic Elderly:

This interview focuses well on the issues defined as the research problem. The length is appropriate, and the informal conversational approach is particularly sensitive to the elderly target population. Although categories and items are well explored, scales are lacking and coding and scoring would be difficult. This would be a good source for items.

The findings from this research are widely cited; they form one of the major data bases in Hispanic elderly research.

Although the authors' permission is required to replicate, this instrument can be obtained at no cost from:

Dr. Marta Sotomayor
1913 Alabaster Drive
Silver Springs, MD 20904
Telephone: (301) 443-3838

A STUDY OF URBAN AND RURAL SPANISH SPEAKING ELDERLY

Description:

This questionnaire was designed to define the needs and the conditions of the urban and rural Spanish-speaking elderly. Areas of the instrument are concerned with support systems, family integration as indicated by family affection, sharing of beliefs, attitudes, opinions and association, adjustment to aging, attitudes toward aging and death, values identification and self-realization, and the utilization of services.

This is a face-to-face interview constructed with open and closed-ended questions, Likert-type scales, and multiple choices. It takes approximately one hour to complete. The interviewers were bicultural, bilingual, and project trained.

The instrument was extensively pretested on elderly Cubans, Puerto Ricans, and Mexicans. The scales have been tested for internal consistency on the basis of test-retest, and split half for reliability, construct and face validity.

The instrument is available in English and Spanish. It is an original construction which was developed in Spanish and then translated to English.

Use with Hispanic Elderly:

The primary purpose of the instrument was to study the Hispanic elderly, although parts have been administered intact to Native Americans and non-minority populations. It is oriented toward a midwestern urban population, and does not reflect adequately the degree of isolation found in more rural areas, nor does it consider differences in language and cultural issues between geographically separated Hispanic subgroups. At times it is wordy and complex. Although it contains many content areas, it lacks in-depth comprehensive assessment of these areas. The health section is inadequate and mental health items are missing. For example, cultural relevance is questionable in that little or no historical data, such as education, occupation, or history of migration, is solicited. Likewise, no specific cultural issues such as ethnic preferences or discrimination are included.

The Spanish-language version is adequate and simply worded, although the vocabulary might not always be appropriate for all subgroups.

Family relations and support systems are covered in-depth, and

88

might be useful as a resource for further research in this area. The length is well within the span of time appropriate and comfortable for an older person.

The author's permission is required for replication; however, there is no fee. The instrument may be obtained from:

Elena Bastida, Ph.D.
Department of Sociology
Wichita State University
Wichita, Kansas 67208
Telephone: (316) 689-3280

CROSS-CULTURAL STUDY OF MINORITY AGED OF
SAN DIEGO (LA PLATICA)

Description:

This is a field methodology allowing interviewers to converse with clients in a friendly and intimate manner while recovering data. The focus is on documenting life styles, values, and coping from the perspective of the Latino elder.

The instrument is a guide in the form of simple questions indicating areas which should be covered during the course of the interview. These areas are: language and background, family, education, employment, problem areas, housing, neighborhood, health, nutrition, transportation, finances, formal and informal supports, and cultural values.

The instrument was administered by a bilingual member of the Hispanic community. Interviewers were trained to consider values of the elderly, language-use patterns, and contextual meanings of the terms used. The interview is long, about 4½ hours, due to inclusion of precontact activity, and observance of culturally appropriate parting rituals which may include partaking of food, gifts, provision of services and mutual assurances, or even the sharing of personal experiences.

The target population was 218 Hispanic elders, Mexican, Puerto Rican, and others from the San Diego area. The reliability of the research instrument is centered on the interviewer's capability to meld the interview guide into the correct local idiom. The instrument needs validation studies.

Use with Hispanic Elderly:

The questionnaire was specifically designed for use with the Hispanic elderly and is particularly sensitive to the social proprieties familiar to this cultural group in their own environment. The issues raised are pertinent to this population, and the method of interview allows for expansion of data collection in any direction, as needed.

Because of its loose design, the most obvious drawback to this instrument is difficulty in recording or coding the information received.

Obviously this is not a regular survey instrument. Despite its drawbacks, this type of instrument could be very useful in minority research where an unusual kind and depth of information is required. It would probably work well as one section of a regular survey where the skillful bilingual interviewer could probe just one issue in-depth.

As an initial survey instrument on a new minority population, it would allow the determination of the appropriate language and issues to be included in the main body of research. It's also ideal for further clarifying issues in case studies.

The use of this instrument requires the author's permission, but it may be obtained at no cost from:

Ramon Valle, Ph.D.
School of Social Work
San Diego State University
San Diego, CA 92182
Telephone: (714) 265-6664

MINORITY ELDERLY EQUITY ASSESSMENT NEEDS SURVEY (MEEANS)

Description:

The purpose of this instrument is to identify the needs, problems, and barriers to benefits and services experienced by the minority elderly. The instrument is a very long questionnaire covering the following areas: language and background, family, education, cultural values, problem areas, housing, neighborhood (social-network scale), transportation, activities of daily living, and instrumental activities of daily living (scale), death, mental health (scale) and life satisfaction (scale).

The original target population was Hispanic (Mexican American) and other minority elderly living in San Diego County. Interviewees were selected by means of a multi-stage, area-probability cluster sampling technique based on data from the 1975 census update.

The design includes open and closed-ended and multiple-choice questions and seven Likert-type scales. It was administered in a face-to-face interview by bilingual or bicultural interviewers trained for the project. It takes approximately 1½ hours to administer.

The instrument is available in English, Spanish, and six other languages: Chinese, Chamorro/Guamanian, Japanese, Korean, Tagalog and Samoan. All language versions were developed in a double-blind process using two native speakers:

1. a "from-English", to native translation was done

2. this native translation was given to a second native speaker for a "back-to-English" translation

3. all "back-to-English" translations were compared with one another and with the original English version of MEEANS for conceptual consistency. All major discrepancies were corrected accordingly. Translators were college-educated native speakers.

The instrument was developed to build on the previous work of Ramon Valle and colleagues using the "platica method" and the "Minority Aged Interview Guide", and to corroborate findings with those of related "equity" projects. It was pretested, and factor analyses were done to investigate validity.

Use with Hispanic Elderly:

Generally the interview questions are insufficient in that they will not generate sufficient data for analysis of the research questions. They lack in-depth information in all areas, for example: the mental-health section does not explore causes of stress, or what elderly do to handle stress in their lives; items on family, marital problems, and chronic illness are absent. Open-ended questions limit reliability and validity. Overall the questionnaire is a potpourri of many other questionnaires.

Specific needs of Hispanics are not addressed, nor are ethnic preferences. Cultural questions are all open-ended, which requires the respondent to define the content of the question, such as...what do you do that is traditional? Culture is addressed in a very abstract way. The language is good, the sensitivity excellent and the style is appealing. This questionnaire is geared to the elderly in general and the oldest cohort specifically. Because of the various ethnic and national groups it surveys, the instrument is of necessity less Hispanic focused.

The instrument is an awkward legal size (8½" x 14"), although another version exists which is in a more convenient format. The authors' permission is required to replicate, and it may be obtained from:

Jose Cuellar
University Center on Aging
6363 Alvarado Court
San Diego, CA 92120
Telephone: (714) 265-6765

OLDER CALIFORNIANS NEEDS ASSESSMENT QUESTIONNAIRE

Description:

This instrument assesses the status, needs and resources of older persons in California. It is structured in a developmental sequence designed to cover major demographic, socioeconomic, and need categories relevant to planning and program evaluation. This categorical sequence should not be altered as reliability and validity could be affected.

The instrument contains 95 items of the fixed-response type, as well as scales of the Guttman and Likert type. Areas covered in the instrument are: home and neighborhood, transportation, health, diet and nutrition, employment, financial status, social concerns, mental health services, information sources, and program utilization. The entire interview averages 53 minutes administration time. Interviewers need not be trained or experienced.

There is no Spanish-language version; all ethnic groups were administered the English version.

The Department of Aging states that the instrument has good item reliability and validity.

The instrument is precoded for 80-column keypunch cards; however, keypunching can be omitted and replaced by direct data entry to disk or tape using standard electronic data processing equipment.

Use with Hispanic Elderly:

This instrument was structured for use with diverse elderly populations, and is not specific for the Hispanic elderly. It does not reflect culturally important issues.

Its greatest insensitivity is its use of exhaustive categories and items on finances. There seems to be far more than necessary in this section.

Generally it is a well-designed instrument which might be useful in further research with the appropriate translations.

Consent for use and the instrument may be obtained from:

Robert A. Harootyan
Special Research Consultant
California Department of Aging
918 J Street
Sacramento, CA 95814
Telephone: (916) 322-3573

A SURVEY OF OLDER PEOPLE - NEW YORK CITY

Description:

This questionnaire is designed to assess the needs of the elderly in the inner city of New York. It covers the areas of: neighborhood, transportation, education, family, living arrangements, life satisfaction (scale), activities of daily living, instrumental activities of daily living, IADL (scale), morale (scale), social networks, employment, income, and service utilization.

The instrument is constructed of 197 items of open and closed and multiple-choice type, and there are Guttman-type scales included. Interviews were conducted in the home in English or Spanish by project trained bilingual interviewers. Administration time is approximately one hour. Although the instrument was translated into Spanish, that version is no longer available.

The instrument was developed as part of a study funded by the AOA and undertaken by the New York City Department of Aging. The population for the study included all persons 60 and over living in the inner city of New York, which turned out to be 47% white, 37% Black and 13% Spanish-speaking of Puerto Rican origin. A replicated probability sample was employed, embodying five randomly selected, stratified, interpenetrating matched samples; the final sample yielded 1,552 respondents representative of older persons living in inner-city neighborhoods in 1970.

Reliability and validity have been determined for the scales incorporated in this instrument.

A.   Family Mutual Aid and Interaction Index

Four broad categories of assistance between child-to-parent and parent-to-child are included: 1) crisis intervention, 2) assistance with chores of daily living, 3) advice giving, and 4) gift giving.

Four separate components of mutual aid are scored through simple summation:

1) parent-to-child dichotomy $(X=2.54)$;
2) parent-to-child frequency $(X=4.23)$;
3) child-to-parent dichotomy $(X=3.85)$; and
4) child-to-parent frequency $(X=6.90)$

The coefficient alpha for the parent-to-child dichotomy was .76; the parent-to-child frequency alpha equaled .78; and for the child-to-parent, dichotomy reliability was .81. The internal consistency

96

of the frequency score was .86. Reliability was computed separately for each ethnic group. The greatest reliability was noted for the Hispanic sample (range of .812 to .892) followed by Blacks (range of .773 to .864) then whites (range of .720 to .833).

Most of these items were incorporated into the "Exchanges of Support and Assistance Index" of the Harris Survey (1975).

B. Familism Index

This is a "scale" consisting of a set of eight items adopted from those of Leichter and Mitchell (1967). The factor scores reflect three dimensions: 1) a proximity factor, i.e., the desirability for young married children and their parents to live close by; 2) a filial obligation factor, i.e., the belief that adult children should help their aged parents, and 3) a kin-oriented factor, i.e., the preferred turning to kin rather than to friends or neighbors to satisfy material or emotional needs. Respondents are asked to agree or disagree with the statements made on a card.

The coefficient alpha for the total sample was .68, which varied from a low of .53 for the Spanish-speaking respondents, to a high of .72 for the Black and .68 for the white elderly.

This scale is one of the few which considers normative aspects of intergenerational relationships. It has been extensively examined through factor analysis.

C. Vulnerability Scale

This measure attempts to assess an individual's probability of institutionalization, or need for community or family based supportive services or both. It is aimed at assessing the level of difficulty experienced by older persons in maintaining themselves in their own homes.

The scale consists of 13 self-report items and one interviewer observation item. Three subscales have been identified: mood, physical health, mobility. The items do not have to be answered in sequential order. (See the table for reliability coefficients.) This scale was correlated with several other tables in order to test discriminate validity. The correlation coefficients were -.63 and .66 with Life Satisfaction, .69 and .74 with the Townsend Incapacity Index, and .95 with the Langer 22-item Mental Status Scale.

Ranges, Means, Standard Deviations, and
Reliability of the Vulnerability Scale

RANGE			Sample 1			Sample 2	
		X	SD	r_{xx}	X	SD	r_{xx}
0-31	TOTAL	7.2	5.50	.74	8.72	5.71	.74
0-14	MOOD	3.46	3.14	.71	4.20	3.27	.69
0-9	MOBILITY	1.42	2.16	.40	1.81	2.35	.43
0-8	HEALTH	2.28	1.98	.57	2.70	1.77	.53

Use with Hispanic Elderly:

This instrument was not directed solely at the Hispanic elderly. It lacks any focus on culturally specific issues; however, with an appropriate translation it could be used as a general needs assessment of any minority group.

The issues facing the urban elderly are scrutinized in-depth and are of equal relevance to all aged cohorts. The section on money and finances is probed deeply and may be difficult for those on assistance to answer. It does seem too long for the average attention span. This is a detailed, comprehensive interview for the elderly, and it could be a model for further research on the Hispanic population with the appropriate Spanish translation.

Copies of and permission to use this instrument may be obtained from:

Mary M. Mayer
City of New York
Office for the Aging
2 Lafayette Street
New York City, NY 10007

IDAHO'S ELDERLY: A NEEDS ASSESSMENT

Description:

The purpose of this instrument was to gather data on conditions of the elderly in Idaho. Areas of inquiry included: demographics, social services, activities, volunteer involvement, housing and neighborhood, diet, health and health care, employment, crime and transportation.

The questionnaire included 110 items—open and closed-ended questions, multiple-choice, completion, and three Likert-type scales.

The instrument is an original construction. Items were provided by project staff and personnel from state agencies involved with services to the elderly.

The sampling design was a random selection of persons 60 years or older throughout Idaho. In all, only 29 interviews out of 2,750 were conducted using the translated Spanish questionnaires. Interviews were conducted face-to-face, and were timed at between 40 and 75 minutes.

Although the instrument was pretested, no information on reliability and validity is given.

Use with Hispanic Elderly:

Hispanics comprised a small number of the total sample (29). The issues, language, and activity levels are geared mainly to the Anglo elderly, and specifically to the young-old and middle-old. The old-old and disabled are not included. The questionnaire is somewhat Idaho specific. A major weakness in its use with minorities is the lack of questions regarding discrimination in the areas of availability of services.

This is a well-designed simple needs assessment for the Anglo elderly of Idaho; it can be obtained at no cost from:

Ken Wildes
Idaho Office on Aging
State House
Boise, Idaho 83720
Telephone: (208) 334-3833

LAS CRUCES NEEDS ASSESSMENT OF THE ELDERLY

Description:

The intent of this instrument was to assess the general service and recreational needs of the elderly, and their utilization of recreational programs in Las Cruces. The section headings cover: general services, transportation, health care, protective services, recreation, social services, housing, and adult education.

The survey is composed of 44 open and closed-ended items. It was administered in Spanish and in English to a 10% random sample of all elderly (50+) in Las Cruces. All interviews were conducted by two employees, one Black and one Hispanic.

The instrument was available as a direct translation from the English, and was, in some cases, translated on the spot into Spanish by the bilingual interviewer. The Spanish version is no longer available.

No specific tests of validity and reliability were performed.

Use with Hispanic Elderly:

This instrument was developed to validate the needs of the elderly in budget sessions, and for grant proposals. It was not specifically developed as a research study, but rather as an evaluation or validation. Use as a rigorous research instrument is limited. The format and organization is simple, lacking depth.

This instrument can be obtained from:

Patsy Yates, Director
Senior Citizens Program
City of Las Cruces
975 So. Mesquite Street
Las Cruces, NM 88001
Telephone: (505) 526-0292

OARS-MULTIDIMENSIONAL-FUNCTIONAL ASSESSMENT
QUESTIONNAIRE (OMFAQ)

Description:

This instrument was originally developed in English by the Older Americans Resources and Services project at the Duke University Center for the Study of Aging. The instrument is designed to assess the extent and degree of impairment of older persons. It measures the respondent's functional level in the areas of social interactions, mental and physical health, and capacity for self-care in daily activities.

OARS was developed primarily for the institutionalized population. It is basically an intake or screening instrument for those needing care in a nursing home, retirement home, or hospital. It is composed of a battery of tests used for placement decisions or to measure progress.

Usually OARS is administered by a team of professionals who have expertise in the section they administer.

Various reliability and validity tests of this instrument have been conducted on Anglo populations.

Two Spanish versions are currently available. Three major studies have used OARS with the Hispanic elderly.

A. Texas Department of Human Resources

The OARS was translated for use with Mexican-American elderly in Texas. The translation is good with the conceptual nuances of the Spanish/English in agreement. This version is adequate for Mexican-Americans; however, care should be taken to insure geographical language differences where appropriate. It has been pretested on the Mexican-American population in Texas.

B. Spanish Family Guidance Center, Coral Gables, Florida

This version of OARS was specifically translated for use with the Cuban elderly. It takes approximately 45 minutes to administer. The Spanish is very readable and generally very good. It has been pretested on the Cuban population.

C. The Well-Being of Older People, Cleveland, Ohio

The English version of OARS was used to assess the impact of Federal programs on the elderly living in Cleveland. A small cohort of English-speaking Hispanics was included in this study, but the individuals are not identified by country of origin.

Use with Hispanic Elderly:

This instrument was originally designed to address the needs and circumstances of the Anglo elderly, and it best suits these purposes. However, it is adequate to investigate these same issues among the Hispanic elderly. The language is appropriate for all groups, provided they are well educated; it would be a problem for those with limited education. The instrument is not sensitive to Hispanic culture in the more complex psychosocial issues such as attitudes toward aging, death, age norms, and roles. The panel of experts thought this instrument should be used with other instruments which are more culturally oriented and which cover cultural and ethnic factors that this instrument misses.

The original source is the Duke University Center for the Study of Aging and Human Development. Duke University's copyright should be displayed as well as the description of the contribution of the Department of Human Resources.

Original Source: The Center for the Study of Aging
and Human Development
Duke University Medical Center
Durham, North Carolina 27710
Telephone: (919) 884-3204

Spanish Version: (for Mexican-Americans)
Gayle Owens, Ph.D.
Director of Evaluation
Planning and Evaluation Division 424-B
P.O. Box 2960
Texas Department of Human Resources
Austin, Texas 78769

Spanish Version: (for Cuban-Americans)
Jose Szapocznik, Ph.D.
Spanish Family Guidance Center
747 Ponce de Leon Blvd., #303
Coral Gables, FL 33134

MULTIPURPOSE SENIOR SERVICES PROJECT CLIENT
ASSESSMENT INSTRUMENT

Description:

This is a multipurpose functional assessment used to determine the social, medical, and psychological needs of the elderly client. The items are from the following areas: family and informal support systems, current services utilization, medical conditions and medications. It also includes a number of scales: activities of daily living (Katz, et al., 1963), instrumental activities of daily living (Lawton and Brady, 1969), short portable mental status questionnaire (Pfeiffer, 1975), life satisfaction (Havinghurst and Neugarten, 1961) and the Cornell Medical Index.

The target population for this study was 1900 elderly and frail clients, 65 years of age or older, drawn from eight sites located throughout California. These clients must qualify for Medi-Cal assistance and have one or more designated disabling conditions. Beyond that, the population is composed of clients from the community, skilled-nursing facilities, and hospitals.

The instrument is an original construction containing open and closed-ended questions, and the five well-known scales designated above. This is a long interview which takes an average of two hours to complete. It is administered face-to-face by nurses and social workers of MSSP staff who have been trained intensively in the program. The East Los Angeles site is the only one which used bicultural and bilingual interviewers exclusively. The instrument has been translated into Spanish; however, it is not designed to assess cultural issues.

There is a large body of literature which reports on the reliability and validity of the scales noted above. Beyond that, interrater reliability tests have been carried out on the entire instrument with a result of over 85% level of agreement.

Use with Hispanic Elderly:

This instrument was not developed to include any minority-specific issues, nor is it able to record minority-specific responses. The Life Satisfaction scale contains items inappropriate to the Hispanic experience, and is very difficult to translate literally. The present Spanish version may not be useful with all subgroups because it is specifically oriented to Mexican elderly in Los Angeles. The content is age appropriate, but the length may be far too long for an elderly person's attention span, particularly for the targeted frail client.

All possible categories are included in this comprehensive questionnaire, which makes it very bulky and perhaps alarming to the client. There are two serious drawbacks to be found in the instrument: the scoring of the ADL is conducted in such a way that the true function level of the client is obscured, and there is an attempt to do a thorough medical assessment through a questionnaire which is neither designed to review the systems of the body, nor geared for recording changes through time in identified diseases or conditions.

Use of this instrument requires the permission of the California Department of Health and Welfare. Copies may be obtained at no cost from:

> Willaim F. Clark
> California Health and Welfare Agency
> 915 Capitol Mall, Room 200
> Sacramento, CA 95814
> Telephone: (916) 322-7200

THE NUECES COUNTY ELDERLY: THEIR MEDICATION
AND PHYSICIANS

Description:

This is a very short instrument devised to gather information about Senior Citizens' problems with medications and their relationships with their physicians.

The survey is an original construction consisting of 20 closed-ended items, half addressing physicians' professional behavior and half addressing medications. One final section allows the respondent to reply in-depth about his or her physician.

The target population was drawn from elderly participating in a Senior Citizens Fair and from a Foster Grandparent Program. The age span of the respondents was 53 to 90 years of age for a total of 169 respondents. This represented an 80% degree of confidence that the study reflected the actual population of that county.

The interviews were administered by project-trained interviewers who were bicultural and bilingual. They translated the instrument into Spanish during face-to-face interviews of approximately 30 minutes. The instrument was subjected to reliability tests for internal consistency.

Use with Hispanic Elderly:

The survey was not designed solely for Hispanics. The items are concerned with gathering very general information on the physicians and medications. Special problems encountered by Hispanics because of unavailability of services or lack of communication in Spanish would not be elicited because response choices are limited and comments cannot be recorded.

The instrument would be more useful if more detailed categories and response choices were included, especially in the delicate area of physician-patient relationships, which is generally a very difficult matter to probe. This is a very important subject for research with the elderly, and this instrument could be expanded and used in further investigations.

The author's permission is required to reproduce the instrument, but it can be obtained at no cost from:

Sandra Gonzalez, Director
Senior Community Services
P.O. Box 9277
Corpus Christi, TX 78408
Telephone: (512) 854-4508

INFORMAL SUPPORTS PROJECT: CLIENT
AND COLLATERAL QUESTIONNAIRES

Description:

These questionnaires help to define the scope of informal services provided by the family, friends, and neighbors. It also surveys the formal services offered by large organizations, governmental and voluntary. It consists of two parts: a client interview and a Collateral questionnaire to be used with those persons named by the client as a support. An integral part of the questionnaire gathers complete data on the following: race/ethnicity, sex, socioeconomic position and health.

Both parts have approximately 110 items which include a number of response types: open and closed-ended, multiple choice, and scales of the Likert and Guttman type. The interviews were conducted by project trained bilingual interviewers. Time for each interview part is approximately one hour.

The instrument was developed by Marjorie Cantor for the Center on Gerontology at Fordham University for use in their project entitled "Impact of the Entry of the Formal Organization on the Existing Informal Networks of Older Americans."

Use with Hispanic Elderly:

This is a very well-designed instrument for use with the elderly. Instructions are clear and precise, it flows well, and scales are available; however, paper size is 8½" x 14" and this makes the questionnaires somewhat unwieldy for face-to-face interviewing. The Spanish language translation is targeted to Puerto Ricans and would require reworking for use among other Hispanic subgroups. This is a good model instrument for measuring informal supports and can be of use in further research in this area. Although the questionnaire is not specifically designed for Hispanics, the instrument is useful for developing additional questionnaires about networks among Hispanic elderly.

It can be obtained along with permission to use from:

Mary Ann Lewis, Ph.D.
Center on Gerontology
Fordham University at Lincoln Center
New York, NY 10023

PROJECTO VIEJITO

Description:

This instrument surveys needs and service utilization of older Hispanics. It assesses the following areas: family relations, utilization of community senior services, attitudes toward government services for the elderly, social contacts, and self-evaluation. It contains Likert-type scales on anomie, morale, and life satisfaction.

The population for this survey was made up of 400 low-income elderly (55+) Blacks, whites, and Hispanics in the urban areas of Ogden and Salt Lake City, Utah. The respondents were identified through door-to-door canvassing.

The Spanish-language instrument is a direct translation from the English version. The questionnaire was administered by project-trained interviewers who were bilingual and bicultural.

The entire instrument was pretested and subjected to tests of reliability and validity.

Use with Hispanic Elderly:

This short instrument is well targeted for the elderly and Hispanics. Items on ethnic identity and politics are excellent, and it specifically addresses issues that might prevent utilization of services. The Spanish-language version is idiomatic and the vocabulary level is aimed at the uneducated. The community panel found this an easy interview to complete. There are a number of typos and translation flaws and the physical size (legal) is awkward, but this is generally a well-done, short and simple questionnaire.

It can be obtained at no cost from:

Dr. Daniel Gallegos
Sociology Department #1208
Weber State College
Ogden, Utah 84408
Telephone: (801) 626-6238

EQUITABLE SHARE IN PUBLIC BENEFITS
BY MINORITY ELDERS

Description:

The purpose of this project was to evaluate the role that cultural attitudes play in the use of public services, the problems encountered in the use of services, and the needs that minority elders may have that are not being met by public services.

Six hundred and twenty-one minority elders in the Washington, D.C. area were surveyed. The sample consisted of 30.8% Black, 10% Hispanic, 18.1% Asian, and 35.9% white respondents. Their ages ranged from 55 to 97.

The questionnaire is available in English only, no translations were developed for the project. The interviewer translated the questionnaire to the respondent as needed in the face-to-face interview.

The instrument is a composite of the RMC Research Corporation's Older American Status and Needs Assessment Questionnaire and additional questions focused on culture.

The questionnaire has been submitted to construct and face validity testing.

Use with Hispanic Elderly:

Little is known about its use with the Hispanic elderly. For further information contact:

David Guttman
The Catholic University of America
Washington, D.C. 20017
Telephone: (202) 635-5461

RETIREMENT RESEARCH PROJECT

Description:

The purpose of this project was to gather data on the opinions and experiences of the elderly with respect to retirement. The questionnaire addresses employment record, retirement activities, feelings about work and retirement, health, family, community participation, service utilization, transportation, housing, and finances.

The questionnaire is a mixture of closed and open-ended items. Some scales are used but they have not been tested for reliability or validity. That testing is currently being completed. The questionnaire was translated into Spanish from English, and back-translated as a reliability check using the double-blind method.

The survey was conducted in Denver, Colorado, and San Diego, California. The interviewers were indigenous to their areas and trained specifically for this survey. They were matched to the respondents on ethnicity, age, and language. The instrument was given in the home of the respondent in a face-to-face interview, lasting approximately 50 minutes.

Use with Hispanic Elderly

This instrument is oriented to the elderly and is culturally sensitive to the Hispanic elderly. While the content is generally good, the extensive use of open-ended items constitutes a coding and analysis problem. Overall, this study could be replicated using a tightened version of this instrument.

The Spanish translation, in the effort to achieve linguistic equivalence, is a bit stiff and formal. A more idiomatic form may be preferrable. The questionnaire is oriented more to Mexican Americans in the Southwest. Modifications would be necessary for use with other Hispanic subgroups as well as in other geographical areas.

The instrument is available to researchers who pay copying and mailing costs. For further information, contact:

Jose Cuellar, Ph.D.
University Center on Aging
6363 Alvarado Court
San Diego, CA 92120
Telephone: (714) 265-6765

FAMILISM AND MORALE IN A RURAL/URBAN SETTING

Description:

This is a survey of the needs and present situation of rural and urban older persons living in northern New Mexico. Concept areas are: community participation, family organization, interaction patterns with immediate and extended family, neighborliness and compadrazgo, mutual aid and affection, service patterns, daily needs, health and morale.

The questionnaire contains 80 open and closed-ended questions and a Spanish translation of Havighurst's Life Satisfaction Index Z. The instrument is in English with a few scattered phrases in Spanish included. It is meant to be administered in a face-to-face interview by indigenous interviewers who are matched on ethnicity, age, and sex and who will use the appropriate language idiom of the interviewee. The interview averages one hour administration time.

The Life Satisfaction Index Z has been subjected to tests of internal consistency to establish reliability, and face validity has been determined.

Use with Hispanic Elderly:

This survey is not sensitive to the cultural issues and problems addressed by elderly Hispanics. Standard items in English used together with local idiomatic Spanish words makes the format appear confusing. The Life Satisfaction Index is geared specifically toward Anglo concepts which have been shown to be rather abstract for most elderly Spanish-speaking people. Familism and morale are surveyed in-depth; however, other categories are treated superficially. The content is specific to the elderly Anglo, and this instrument could be a source for items in that area.

The author's permission is required to use this instrument, but it can be obtained at no charge from:

Dr. Alvin O. Korte
New Mexico Highlands University
Las Vegas, NM 87701
Telephone: (505) 425-3198

Description:

The purpose of the instrument is to gather data from a cross ethnic sample of the elderly in Los Angeles on a variety of issues affecting them, such as: health, housing, economics, crime, transportation, political participation, and so forth.

The interview schedule contains 92 items which are clustered in four domains. These domains are used in the separate construction of specific attitudinal scales and are 1) attitudes toward the aged; 2) attitudes toward civil disobedience; 3) attitudes toward government responsibility for the aged; 4) health-incapacity index.

The research design was a comparative study of Black, Mexican-American, and white aged in many social and cultural contexts. It addressed the life situations of aging populations with a view toward influencing national policy. The sample was a stratified probability sample in which the objective was to obtain 400 respondents in each ethnic and social category as well as 400 in the following age strata: 45-54, 55-64, and 65-74.

The interviewers were project trained and matched on ethnicity, race, and the language preference of the respondents. All interviewers were over 35 years of age. Mexican Americans had to be bilingual and fluent in reading, writing, and speaking Spanish. Interviews were conducted in the respondents' homes.

The instrument was predominately closed-ended questions. Hand cards are used extensively. The interview time averages 75 minutes. Reliability and validity tests were not performed. Scales were formulated on the white sample, and thus do not provide validation across subcultures.

The instrument is available in English and Spanish. The translation was provided by university-based translators and includes the Mexican-American idiom. The interview was back-translated twice into Spanish, and special attention was paid to interviewer comments regarding meaning for respondents. Reliability and face validity of the Spanish version has been established.

Use with Hispanic Elderly:

This questionnaire was not intended solely for this specific ethnic group, thus it lacks a certain amount of cultural appropriateness in items. The panel of experts thought the instrument was more oriented toward the middle-class Anglo, and that this was reflected in the level of language used and the complexity of questions. It is entirely urban oriented since this is the target group.

It attempts to cover many areas; thereby covering none in-depth. This instrument has served as a model because it was among the first that focused on the elderly. The panel considered this one of the better instruments because of clarity, single focus of items, good formatting, and clear directions. It is useful as a source for items, but additional items would be required for all topics.

This instrument is not copyrighted nor does it require the author's permission to use. It may be obtained from:

Pauline K. Ragan
Andrus Gerontology Center
Laboratory for Social Organization and
  Behavior
University of Southern California
Los Angeles, CA 90007

SURVEY OF CRIME AND THE ELDERLY

Description:

This is a telephone survey of neighborhood crime and its effects on the elderly. The instrument is designed to provide a profile of the victimization experiences and fears of older residents, their home and personal security practices, and their awareness of crime prevention and assistance activities in their neighborhood and city.

The areas covered in the survey are: neighborhood interaction, policy protection, crime-prevention programs and utilization, types of crime, personal response to crime, neighborhood environment, home safety, housing, income, and personal demographics.

The instrument is available in both English and Spanish. It contains 108 closed-ended items. The instrument is an original construction. Both English and Spanish versions were extensively pretested. No tests of reliability or validity were reported.

Professional, project-trained interviewers were used to administer this questionnaire by telephone in an average time of 25 minutes.

The study population consisted of persons, aged 60 and over, living in New York, Milwaukee, New Orleans, and Los Angeles. Systematic probability sampling of city directories was used to define this population. While Hispanic elderly were not the target population, they were represented in the total sample.

Use with Hispanic Elderly:

This instrument is rather superficial and is not specific to the Hispanic experience. The community panel found the response choices too limited, again indicating the superficiality of the instrument.

Because of the superficiality of content, this instrument is of limited use; however, it can be adapted for a general survey.

The authors' permission is required to replicate. The instrument may be obtained from:

William Klecka
George F. Bishop
Behavioral Science Laboratory
University of Cincinnati
Cincinnati, Ohio 45221

MINNESOTA MULTIPHASIC PERSONALITY INVENTORY (MMPI)

Description:

The MMPI is a 550-item inventory of statements to be answered as true or false. The purpose of this inventory is to assess personality structure.

The MMPI is a standard instrument that has been widely used in 45 countries and translated in 70 languages. Extensive reliability and validity testing has been and continues to be undertaken.

One obvious problem has been the assurance of linguistic and conceptual equivalence across all populations. Additionally, items must be considered in cultural contexts. This continues to elicit controversy about this particular inventory.

This instrument is self-administered and may take from two to three hours to complete.

Use with Hispanic Elderly:

As with all instruments of this kind, there are some obvious problems with administration of the MMPI to Hispanic elderly. These include: fatigue, other physiological shortcomings, educational levels providing problems of reading and interpretation, accuracy of interpretation by a clinician, and general questions of the applicability of this instrument to Hispanics who are less acculturated to American life than the group used as the standard. Validity for Hispanic elderly residing in the United States with low degrees of acculturation is questionable. In fact, some evidence exists that suggests that persons other than Anglos tend to score in ranges that approach pathology since the Anglo norm is used as the standard.

For further information, contact:

James H. Butcher, Ph.D.
Department of Psychology
N438 Elliot Hall
75 East River Road
Minneapolis, MN 55455
Telephone: (612) 373-4164

HISPANIC VETERANS: HEALTH CARE UTILIZATION

Description:

The purpose of this study was to evaluate the health-care seeking behavior of Hispanic veterans residing in the Los Angeles area. The questionnaire addresses military participation, health care use (specifically the Veterans Administration), satisfaction with health care, perceptions of treatment, and barriers to health care.

The questionnaire includes 45 closed-ended items. Included are scales measuring health-care satisfaction, health beliefs, health outlook, and health perceptions. Extensive reliability and validity testing were conducted on these scales (see John Ware, Health Services Research, Winter, Vol. 11, #4).

The questionnaire is available in both English and Spanish. It is an original construction, drawing some items from other health surveys. The translation is from English to Spanish and back-translated.

The sample of 559 veterans was selected using a multi-stage probability sampling design. The sample represented the three major war eras; 10% were 60+.

The interviewers were all bilingual and bicultural males; however, fewer than 5% of the veterans selected Spanish as the language of preference. Administration time is approximately one hour.

Use with Hispanic Elderly:

The questionnaire is primarily veteran oriented and less Hispanic or age oriented. While many questions address cultural issues they are primarily for assessing their role in health care use. This questionnaire is not particularly useful to research with the Hispanic elderly. Its primary use may be in the overall health questions and scales.

The instrument is available from:

Milton Greenblatt, M.D.
NPI
University of California
Los Angeles, CA 90024
Telephone: (213) 825-9548

A SPANISH LANGUAGE COMPUTER DERIVED
MENTAL HEALTH RATING

Description:

This scale was devised to measure mental distress. It consists of 22 items. Nine items are from the 22-item Langner Screening Scale (Langner, 1962). A psychological distress score for each individual is computed by summing up the number of symptomatic responses.

The scale was originally developed in English, in connection with the Midtown Manhattan Restudy (Srole, 1975; Singer, et al., 1976). It was later translated into Spanish by Kyriakos Markides of the University of Texas Health Science Center for use in a project concerned with investigating the differences in psychological distress between elderly Mexican Americans and Anglos.

The scale is constructed totally of fixed-response items. It was administered to Mexican-American and Anglo subjects in their preferred language by bilingual Mexican-American interviewers. The scale takes about 10 minutes to administer.

The sample used was a probability stratified random sample based on ethnicity and sex in San Antonio, Texas, from the 1970 census count.

The Spanish-language scale has been subjected to tests of predictive and face validity only.

Use with Hispanic Elderly:

This is an attempt to develop a short quantifiable rating of mental health. The items are stated simply and are general enough to be used with all subgroups of Hispanics. It includes a wide spectrum of items on distress and includes loneliness and paranoia. The Spanish translation overall is good; however, some verb forms have been changed and the scale is not an exact English equivalent. Asking about nervous breakdown in the first question is somewhat insensitive; however, there are no other major drawbacks to this scale.

Permission to use the Spanish version CMHR and a copy can be obtained from:

Kyriakos S. Markides
The University of Texas
Health Science Center at San Antonio
7703 Floyd Curl Drive
San Antonio, TX 78284
Telephone: (512) 691-6391

Computer Derived Mental Health Rating in Singer, E., Cohen, S.M. Garfinkel, R., and Srole, L. 1976. Replicating Psychiatric Ratings through Multiple Regression Analysis: The Midtown Manhattan Restudy. Journal of Health and Social Behavior, 17, 376-387.

Srole, L., 1975, Measurement and Classification in Psychiatric Epidemiology. Journal of Health and Social Behavior, 16, 347-364.

Langner, T.S., 1962. A Twenty-two Items Screening Score of Psychiatric Symptoms Indicating Impairment. Journal of Health and Social Behavior, 3, 269-276.

NATIONAL SURVEY OF PEOPLE OF MEXICAN DESCENT
IN THE UNITED STATES

Description:

This instrument is a comprehensive nationwide survey of Chicano heads-of-household or spouses of heads of Mexican descent. "Mexican descent" is defined as a person who reports any two of his or her grandparents as being solely of Mexican ancestry. The purpose of the research is: 1) to assess the mental-health implications of ethnic identification, identity, and consciousness among persons of Mexican origin; and 2) to empirically assess the major areas of life of the Mexican-American population such as work attitudes and labor-force participation, family-related phenomena, language, behavior, and attitudes.

The sampling design is a national multistage-probability sampling design based on 1970 U.S. Population Census Fifth Count tapes. Interviewers are bicultural and bilingual, trained by the project.

The instrument is constructed with both open and closed-ended questions, Likert-type scales, and vignettes. Interviewing is conducted in a three-and-a-half hour face-to-face session.

The instrument is available in English and Spanish. Linguistic and conceptual equivalence were determined by back-translation. The scales have been submitted to tests of internal consistency for reliability and construct and face validity tests.

Use with Hispanic Elderly:

The questionnaire is not intended for this specific age group, thus many sections are inappropriate to the elderly. Specific questions addressing the concerns of the aged are not asked or are only superficially addressed. Many questions call for great detail, which may present problems for the aged cohort. The length of the interview may prohibit use with this population. The instrument does not appear to capture rural/urban differences or geographical differences. Grammatical constructions and transitions to many content areas are likely to confuse the elderly. The instrument could be useful as a resource in the development of other questionnaires specific to the Mexican elderly.

The use of the instrument requires the author's permission. Copies may be obtained at no expense from:

Carlos Arce
Institute for Social Research
The University of Michigan
Ann Arbor, Michigan 48105
Telephone: (313) 764-9300

ACCULTURATION BEHAVIORAL SCALE

Description:

This instrument measures levels of individual acculturation by testing the dimensions of behavior and values. It is primarily targeted to Cuban Americans.

The questionnaire consists of two sections. The first is a self-reported behavior section containing 24 items prepared in a five-point Likert format with eight items on language, seven items on daily customs or habits and nine items on idealized lifestyle. The second section consists of six problem situations related to value orientations.

The items are scored using unit weights, and the person's total score is the simple sum of the 24 weighted responses. Total scores on the behavioral scale can range from 24 to 120 with a total score of 24 indicating minimum acculturation.

This instrument has been administered to 265 Cubans and 201 Anglos residing in Miami, Florida. The age range was 14 to 85 years and it took approximately 5-10 minutes per person to administer.

The scale has been submitted to reliability and validity testing. The discriminant item validity test showed a significant item discrimination both between Cubans and the cultural-reference groups, and between high and low-acculturated Cubans.

Tests for internal consistency on the behavioral and value-acculturation scales showed a coefficient alpha of .97 and .77 respectively. On the test-retest measurement, the behavioral and value acculturation scales' correlation was .96 and .86 respectively.

The instrument is available in both English and Spanish.

Use with Hispanic Elderly:

This instrument is very short and easy to administer. It captures more than one dimension: behavior and values. It is in its present form oriented towards Cubans, but with modifications it could be used with other groups.

With regard to use with the elderly, it is not age focused, seeming to have greater utility with a younger cohort.

For additional information contact:

David Santisteban, Ph.D.
Associate Director
Spanish Family Guidance Center
747 Ponce de Leon Blvd., Suite 303
Coral Gables, FL 33134

ACCULTURATION RATING SCALE FOR
MEXIC AN-AMERICANS (ARSMA)

Description:

This scale is a 20-item, closed-ended questionnaire that measures the degree of acculturation among Mexican Americans. The scale is able to differentiate five distinct types of Mexican Americans based on the level of acculturation: very Mexican, Mexican-oriented bicultural, "true" bicultural, Anglo-oriented bicultural, and very Anglicized.

This scale is easily scored. The scores (1-5) for each question are summed and a mean is calculated to derive the scale score that corresponds to one of the five distinct types. ARSMA may be given in English, Spanish or both languages depending on the preference of the respondent.

Reliability and validity measures have been calculated for this scale. A coefficient alpha of .88 was obtained measuring internal validity for an N=134. The test-retest coefficient of stability was .72. Additionally, validity tests were done. These include construct, face, and discriminant validity measures.

Administration time is approximately 10-15 minutes. It can be administered in any mode that is convenient: self, group, face-to-face interview, mail, and so forth. It is specifically designed to allow for someone other than the respondent to complete on the basis of informant information, observational data, and rater judgment. For this reason, it is particularly applicable to disturbed patients or individuals whose self-report may be unreliable.

Use with Hispanic Elderly:

The major problem with the instrument is it is uni-dimensional. It does require supplementation with other variables to gain a broader picture of acculturation. Because of the types of questions asked, it is only applicable to Mexican Americans, but it could be modified to address other Hispanic subgroups. The scale is not age-limited; therefore, the use of this scale is as applicable to the elderly as to any other group.

An additional problem is the simplistic weighting of each item and the equal weighting regardless of the importance of the item to the acculturation process.

The strengths of the instrument are that it is short and easy to administer, provides a general measurement of cultural learning but not specific to any area, for example, attitudes and beliefs, or practices and preferences.

For further information on this instrument contact:

Israel Cuellar, Ph.D.
San Antonio State Hospital
P.O. Box 23310
San Antonio, TX 78223
Telephone: (512) 532-8811

CUBAN BEHAVIORAL IDENTITY QUESTIONNAIRE

Description:

The purpose of this instrument is to assess the degree of Cuban ethnic identity.

The instrument is a short eight-item questionnaire answerable in a seven point Likert-scale format. It inquires about the frequency with which respondents engage in several ethnic behaviors, and the degree to which they are familiar with Cuban idiomatic expressions and Cuban artists and musicians.

The instrument demonstrates a high degree of internal consistency (alpha = .84). While there are no significant differences on most demographic characteristics, there are significant differences with respect to age at time of arrival, years of residence in the U.S., and Cuban density of the neighborhood of residence. For further discussion on the development of this questionnaire see: Margarita Garcia and Leonor I. Lega "Development of a Cuban Ethnic Identity Questionnaire" Hispanic Journal of Behavioral Sciences, Vol. 1, No. 3, 247-261.

Use with Hispanic Elderly:

This is a well-designed, short instrument for assessing Cuban identity. There seems to be some problems in assessment as related to the elderly. With respect to other groups the questionnaire is not so easily transferrable. In essence, if it is to be used with another Hispanic subgroup, the researcher would almost have to embark on the same extensive procedure used by the author to sort out the appropriate questions.

For further information, contact:

Dr. Margarita Garcia
Dept. of Psychology
Montclair State College
Upper Montclair, NJ 07043
Telephone: (201) 893-5201

LEISURE TIME

Description:

The purpose of this 1970 survey was to assess leisure time and mental-health functioning, focusing on age and life-stage as key variables that shape leisure choices and satisfactions. The sample included 1441 persons (Anglo, Black, and Mexican American) stratified by sex, ethnicity, two-family occupational status levels, and sex/age groups, of which 460 were 65+. The survey was conducted in Houston, Texas.

The survey was conducted by NORC (University of Chicago). The interviewers were matched on ethnicity and age group as well as language preference.

The instrument is administered in a two hour face-to-face interview consisting of predominately closed-ended questions. It includes one section to be self-administered.

The instrument is available in both English and Spanish; however, the Spanish version has the questions in Spanish and the responses in English. The questions were translated to Spanish from the original English. Predictive and construct validity tests were performed on selected items.

Use with Hispanic Elderly:

The content on leisure-time use is good, but it does tend to be specific to Houston with regard to places and activities. It is not Hispanic nor age oriented. In most respects, it is more oriented to younger cohorts, even though the topic is appropriate to the aged.

The Spanish translation is too academic and not suitable for Mexican elderly. Overall the translation is understandable, but not very good.

The elderly panel found the self-administered section difficult due to language and educational levels (lack of sufficient reading skills, vision, understanding of tasks, and so forth).

Overall, the specific items on leisure-time use and activities can provide a good resource for questionnaire development for Mexican elderly.

For the author's permission to use, and to obtain a copy of the instrument, contact:

Charles Gaitz or Judith Scott
Texas Research Institute of
  Mental Sciences
1300 Moursund Avenue
Houston, TX 77030
Telephone: (713) 797-1976

CHAPTER IV

CONSIDERATIONS FOR HISPANIC
GERONTOLOGICAL RESEARCH

As indicated by the limited number of instruments identified, very few instruments have been developed specifically for the Hispanic elder. Spanish language instruments which have been tested for reliability and validity are even rarer. Most of the instruments which are available have been developed recently. As new instruments become available, we can expect a new level of sophistication as a result of the greater emphasis being placed on the conduct of reliability and validity tests, providing a greater pool of standardized items in the future.

Currently, a high level of communication within the field of Hispanic research provides a medium for idea exchange. Several universities now have Hispanic Research Centers which publish and widely disseminate information on current developments in the field. This network is a valuable resource for communicating diverse approaches to research in the Hispanic community. In addition, several journals now exist that focus on the Hispanic and provide a system for evaluating existing instruments and methodological issues.

Significantly, some suggestions for conducting surveys among minority groups and, in particular, among the Hispanic elderly have evolved in the process of evaluating the instruments for this project. In general, research focusing on Hispanics must control for cultural bias; therefore, research design and implementation must reflect techniques sensitive to this issue. Recently, minority and majority researchers have been much more willing to critique their own past efforts in the interest of illuminating major methodological oversights related to the control of cultural bias. Self-criticism provides important insights both to the researcher and to others so that the same problems do not continue to occur. Self-criticism and criticism of others are the difficult consequences of being a researcher; however, to ensure progress in the arena of Hispanic research, we must continue to pursue better and more innovative methodologies that only the process of the critique can generate. Thus, the more we are able to minimize cultural bias (it can never be totally eliminated), the less open to criticism we will be in the scientific and Hispanic communities.

One area that would lend itself to enhancing other researchers' knowledge in the field would be a more complete discussion of the research methodology in the reports produced by principal investigators. In reviewing the reports submitted on numerous studies cited in this review of instruments, the following areas were either omitted or only cursorily addressed.

A. Methods:

1. Sampling:

    *limited discussion of sample selection criteria, who was included or excluded. Why a particular region for sample selection and specific Hispanic group(s) targeted.

2. Instrument Translation:

    *specific idiom of language
    *assurance of equivalence (e.g. backtranslation, panel, etc.)
    *information on whether or not the instrument was developed specifically for Hispanics and in cases where it was not, what methods were undertaken to insure minimization of cultural bias.

3. Analytical Approaches:

    *reliability and validity tests, which tests were used, what were the outcomes, if tests were conducted on parts of the instrument, which ones, etc.
    *specific statistical techniques used to analyze the data

B. Discussion:

1. Often the results of the data were reported but not interpreted. What did the data show? What does it mean? Why is it important? Inferences beyond the data were often not presented as such, thus the reader was not sure if the data showed this fact or if it was drawn from experience. Of what use is this to other researchers?

2. What limitations were there in the conduct of the study? If there were problems in the conduct of the research, how were they handled and what might others learn from this work to be used in other similar works?

We have much to learn from each other and often one source of information is the reviewing of final reports of other projects. The greater care we take in delineating our methods, both those which are successful and those which are not, the greater the contribution to each other.

The Instruments

Those who develop questionnaires for research know only too well that there are no perfect questionnaires. They all have problems in some fashion or another. Few researchers are entirely satisfied with the questionnaire they have developed; most can reflect back after the research is completed and think about what they could have done better. There are a few key flaws that can be avoided, however, if the questionnaire is carefully field-tested. Other pitfalls which showed up on many of the instruments evaluated that should be avoided included:

1. overlapping categories in response categories

2. more than one question being asked in a single question

3. response categories that did not fit the question when asked of Hispanics, or reflected regional differences

4. Spanish translations inappropriate to the Hispanic target group

5. equivalences (conceptual, contextual, or linguistic) were not appropriate

6. ambiguity of questions

7. the ordering of questions were not sensitive to Hispanic cultural norms

8. age cohort differences were not reflected in the response categories

9. length of the questionnaire did not consider attention or fatigue factor

10. need of greater use of follow-up (branching questions) to clarify meaning of stem question response

As a result of this project, existing available research instruments which have been used for researching the Hispanic elderly have been identified. Here, we have attempted to bring together as much as is currently known in the research of this particular target group.

The methodological issues identified provide a means for bringing together a variety of viewpoints and for generating new ideas on which future research can capitalize and expand. It is hoped that the dissemination of this information will contribute to the ongoing dialogue in this area of research and that consistent methodologies will emerge which further enhance the quality and quantity of Hispanic research, particularly as it pertains to the elderly.

APPENDIX

PROJECT METHODOLOGY

The overall goal of this project was to identify and assess available research instruments in the Spanish and English language and identify methodological issues related to research on the Hispanic elderly.

In order to achieve this goal an inventory of available research instruments in Spanish and English useful for conducting policy, planning and programming relevant research on all groups of Hispanic elderly were gathered by the following procedures:

1) project staff consulted with other researchers in the field to gather names and addresses of researchers who potentially had or knew of instruments administered to the Hispanic elderly.

2) a list of contacts was developed and a letter was sent requesting questionnaires in both English and Spanish (if available), all reports, manuals and articles related to the instrument and any additional information on any other instruments, research projects, or persons who knew of additional instruments.

3) project staff continued to follow up on all potential informants and sent out additional letters requesting information as new leads provided.

4) a literature review was conducted by project staff to identify published research reports involving survey instrumentation to study the Hispanic elderly. An additional focus of the literature review was to provide a framework for assessing the state of the art for identification of gaps and methodological issues.

To review and evaluate the gathered instruments, a panel of experts was recruited. Selection of this panel was based upon the following criteria: area of research expertise, ethnic specialization and geographical familiarity.

The following researchers were selected:

Name	Ethnic Specialty	Geographic Representation	Research Expertise
a) Elena Bastida University of Kansas	Cuban/ Puerto Rican	Kansas	English language Instrument bank AOA
b) David Maldonado University of Texas, Houston	Mexican American	Texas	Research Methodology
c) Phillip Garcia University of Michigan	Mexican American	Michigan	Survey Research
d) David Mangen University of Southern California	Anglo	California	Research Methodology
e) David Santisteban University of Miami	Cuban	Florida	Survey Research
f) Ray Valle San Diego State University	Mexican/ Cuban	California	Ethno Methodology

Each instrument was rated independently and recorded on rating sheets which were collected prior to any group discussion. This process, called the Delphi Method, allowed for testing the reliability of the responses of the experts. The panel was asked to rate the instruments on the following areas:

A. Technical Aspects: format, design, type of print, size of the instrument, clarity of interviewer instructions, ease of coding.

B. Age Appropriateness: relevance to the elderly and elderly age subgroups.

C. Cultural Appropriateness: relevance to Hispanic culture and the culture of Hispanic subgroups.

D. Language Appropriateness: linguistic equivalence, appropriate-ness of the translation for Hispanic subgroups, and conceptual/contextual equivalence.

134

E. Content Appropriateness: appropriateness of the substantive
   area, department of inquiry, appropriateness of questions.

   A second panel of community members was also recruited. This
panel was made up of four individuals in the age cohorts 55-60, 61-65,
66-70, 70+. They represented the following groups: Mexican American,
Mexican national, Puerto Rican, and Cuban. Two were Spanish speakers
only and two were bilingual in English and Spanish. They were given
various parts of selected questionnaires and asked to comment on their
appropriateness to the elderly in general, the specific ethnic group
targeted, the age cohort they represented; further they were urged
to give feedback generally from their own perspectives about the
instrument.

   The combined input from all sources - the panel of researchers,
the panel of community elders, literature researches, and the experience
of the investigators - have lead to the development of this document.

BIBLIOGRAPHY

Atchley, R.C. "Respondents vs. Refusers in an Interview Study of Retired Women: An Analysis of Selected Characteristics," Journal of Gerontology, Vol. 24, No. 1, 1969, pp. 42-47.

Bell, D.; Kaschau, P.; and Zellman, G. Delivering Services to Elderly Members of Minority Groups: A Critical Review of the Literature, (Santa Monica, CA.: The Rand Corporation), 1976.

Bengtson, V.L.; Cuellar, J.B.; and Ragan, P.K. "Stratum Contrasts and Similarities in Attitudes Toward Death," Journal of Gerontology, Vol. 32, No. 1, 1977, pp. 76-88.

Bengtson, V.L. "Ethnicity and Aging: Problems and Issues in Current Social Science Inquiry," in Ethnicity and Aging: Theory, Research and Policy, Gelfard, D.E. and Kutzik, A.J. (eds.), (New York: Springer Publishing), 1979, pp. 9-31.

Bengtson, V.L., et al. "Relating Academic Research to Community Concerns: A Case Study in Collaborative Efforts," The Journal of Social Issues, Vol. 33, No. 4, 1977, pp. 75-92.

Bengtson, V.L. and Ragan, P.K. "Aging Among Blacks, Mexican-Americans and Whites; Development, Procedures, and Results of the Community Survey," Andrus Gerontology Center, University of Southern California, NSF Grant APR-75-21178, 1977.

Bengtson, V.L. and Burton, L. "Familism, Ethnicity and Supports Systems: Patterns of Contrast and Congruence," A Paper presented at the Western Gerontological Association, San Diego, CA., 1980.

Blauner, R. and Wellman, D. "Toward the Decolonization of Social Research," in The Death of White Sociology, Lardner, J.A. (ed.), (New York: Vintage Books), 1973.

Bloom, D. and Padilla, A. "A Peer-Interviewer Model for Conducting Surveys Among Mexican-American Youth," University of California, Spanish Speaking Mental Health Research Center, Los Angeles, CA., Occasional Paper #8, 1979.

Brislin, R.W. "Back-translation for Cross-cultural Research," Journal of Cross-Cultural Psychology, Vol. 1, No. 2, 1970, pp. 185-216.

Brislin, R.W.; Lonner, W.J.; and Thorndike, R.M. Cross-cultural Research Methods, (New York: Wiley-Interscience), 1973.

Cantor, M.H. "Effect of Ethnicity on Life Styles of the Inner-City Elderly," in Community Planning for an Aging Society: Designing Services and Facilities, Lawton, P.; Newcomer, R.; and Byertz, T., (Stroudsberg, PA.: Dowden, Hutchinson and Ross, Inc.), 1976.

Cantor, M. and Meyer, M. "Health and the Inner-city Elderly," The Gerontologist, Vol. 16, No. 1, 1976, pp. 17-24.

Carp, F.M. Factors in the Utilization of Services by Mexican-American Elderly, (Palo Alto, CA.: American Institute for Research), 1968.

Carp, F.M. "Housing and Minority Group Elderly," The Gerontologist, Vol. 9, No. 1, 1969, pp. 20-24.

Clark, J.M. "Los Cubanos de la isla y del Exilio: Un Analisis socio-demografico comparativo," in Los Cubanos en los Estados Unidos, Herrera, M.C.; Szapocznik, J.; and Rasco, J.I. (eds.), (Miami: Universal Press), 1979.

Crouch, B.M. "Age and Institutional Support: Perceptions of Older Mexican-Americans," Journal of Gerontology, Vol. 27, No. 4, 1972, pp. 524-529.

Cuellar, J.B. "Ethnographic Methods: Studying Aging in an Urban Mexican-American Community," A Paper presented at the Western Gerontological Association, Portland, Oregon, October, 1974.

Cuellar, J.B. "The Senior Citizen's Club: The Older Mexican-American in the Voluntary Association," in Life's Career: Aging, Meyerhoff, B.G. and Simic, A. (eds.), (Beverly Hills, CA.: Sage Publications), 1978, pp. 207-229.

de Arma, E.D. "The Super-System and the Spanish-Speaking Elderly," in Proceedings of the Puerto Rican Conference on Human Services, Curren, D.J. et. al. (eds.), National Coalition of Spanish Speaking Mental Health Organizations, Washington, D.C., 1975, pp. 169-178.

Dieppa, M.D. Retirement: A Differential Experience for Mexican Americans and Anglos, unpublished Doctoral Dissertation, University of Denver, Denver, Colorado, 1977.

Donaldson, E. and Martinez, E. "The Hispanic Elderly of East Harlem," Aging, Nos. 305-306, March-April, 1980, pp. 6-11.

Dowd, J.D. and Ragan, P.K. "Nonresponse in an Aged Sample: A Cross-Ethnic Comparison," in Socio-cultural Contexts of Aging: Implications of Social Policy, University of Southern California, The Andrus Gerontology Center, 1974.

138

Dowd, J.D. and Bengtson, V.L. "Aging in Minority Populations: An Examination of the Double Jeopardy Hypothesis," Journal of Gerontology, Vol. 33, No. 3, 1978, pp. 427-436.

Estrada, L. The Spanish Origin Elderly: A Demographic Survey, 1970-1975, unpublished manuscript of the Population Division, U.S. Bureau of the Census, 1976.

Grebler, L.; Moore, J.W.; and Guzman, R.C. The Mexican-American People: The Nation's Second Largest Minority, (New York: The Free Press), 1970.

Gurland, B., et al., "The Comprehensive Assessment and Referral Evaluation (CARE) -- Rationale, Development, and Reliability," International Journal of Aging and Human Development, Vol. 8, No. 1, 1977, pp. 9-42.

Kahana, E. and Felton, B.L. "Social Context and Personal Need: A Study of Polish and Jewish Aged," The Journal of Social Issues, Vol. 33, No. 4, 1977, pp. 56-74.

Keefe, S.E.; Padilla, A.M.; and Carlos, M.L. "The Mexican-American Extended Family as an Emotional Support System," Human Organizations, Vol. 38, No. 2, 1979, pp. 144-152.

Korte, A.O. Social Interaction and the Morale of Spanish-Speaking Elderly, unpublished Doctoral Dissertation, School of Social Welfare, University of Denver, Denver, Colorado, 1978.

Korte, A.O. "Theoretical Perspectives in Mental Health and the Mexicano Elders," in Chicano Aging and Mental Health, Miranda, M. and Ruiz, R.A. (eds.), Washington, D.C., NIMH, USDHHS, 81-952, 1981, pp. 1-37.

Kuder, G.F. and Richardson, M.W. "The Theory of the Estimation of Test Reliability," Psychometrika, No. 2, 1937, pp. 151-160.

Laurel, N. An Intergenerational Comparison of Attitudes Toward the Support of Aged Parents: A Study of Mexican-Americans in two South Texas Communities, unpublished Doctoral Dissertation, School of Social Work, University of Southern California, Los Angeles, CA., 1976.

Leonard, O.E. "The Older Rural Spanish People of the Southwest," in Older Rural Americans, Youmans, E.G. (ed.), (Lexington: University of Kentucky Press), 1967, pp. 239-261.

Lindholm, K.J.; Marin, G.; and Lopez, R.E. "Fundamentals of Proposal Writing: A Guide for Minority Researchers," National Institute of Mental Health, Center for Minority Group Mental Health Programs, Rockville, MD., 1980.

Maldonado, D. "The Chicano Aged," Social Work, Vol. 20, No. 3, pp. 213-216.

Manuel, R.C. and Bengtson, V.L. "Ethnicity and Family Patterns in Mature Adults: Effects of Race, Age, SES, and Sex," a Paper presented at the Pacific Sociological Association, San Diego, CA., 1976.

Markides, K.S. "Ethnic Differences in Age Identification," Social Science Quarterly, Vol. 60, No. 4, 1980, pp. 659-666.

Martinez, M.Z. "Family Policy for Mexican-Americans and Their Aged," The Urban and Social Change Review, Vol. 12, No. 2, 1979, pp. 16-19.

McConnell, S., et al. "No Gold Watch: The Retirement Experiences of Older Blacks and Mexican-Americans," Andrus Gerontology Center, University of Southern California, Los Angeles, CA., 1979.

Miranda, M. "Latin American Culture and American Society: Contrasts," in the National Conference on the Spanish-Speaking Elderly, Hernandez, A. and Mendoza, J. (eds.), (Kansas City: National Chicano Social Planning Council), 1975.

Montero, D. "Research Among Racial and Cultural Minorities: An Overview," The Journal of Social Issues, Vol. 33, No. 4, 1977, pp. 1-10.

Montiel, M. "The Mexican-American Family: A Proposed Research Framework," Proceedings from the First National Conference on Spanish-Speaking Elderly, Shawnee Mission, Kansas, 1975.

Moore, J.W. The Mexican-Americans, (Inglewood Cliffs, N.J.: Prentice-Hall, Inc.), 1970.

Moore, J.W. "Situational Factors Affecting Minority Aging," The Gerontologist, Vol. 11, No. 1, part 2, 1971, pp. 88-93.

Moore, J.W. "Social Constraints on Sociological Knowledge: Academics and Research Concerning Minorities," Social Problems, Vol. 21, 1973, pp. 64-77.

Moore, J.W., et al. Homeboys: Gangs, Drugs, and Prison in the Barrios of Los Angeles, (Philadelphia: Temple University Press), 1978.

Myers, V. "Survey Methods for Minority Populations," The Journal of Social Issues, Vol. 33, No. 4, 1977, pp. 11-19.

Newquist, D., et al. Prescription for Neglect: Experiences of Older Blacks and Mexican Americans with the American Health Care System, Andrus Gerontology Center, University of Southern California, Los Angeles, CA., 1979.

Newton, F.C. and Ruiz, R.A. "Chicano Culture and Mental Health Among the Elderly," in Chicano Aging and Mental Health, Miranda, M. and Ruiz, R.A. (eds.), Washington, D.C., NIMH, USDHHS, 81-952, 1981, pp. 38-75.

Newton, F.C. "Issues in Research and Service Delivery Among Mexican American Elderly: A Concise Statement with Recommendations," The Gerontologist, Vol. 20, No. 2, 1980, pp. 208-213.

Nunez, F. Variations of Fulfillment of Expectations of Social Intervention and Morale Among Aging Mexican-Americans and Anglos, unpublished MA thesis, Dept. of Psychology, University of Southern California, 1975.

Nunez, F. "Perceptual Family Structure and Functions Among Mexican-American and Anglos in Crisis," unpublished manuscript, 1977.

Nunnally, J. Psychometric Theory, (New York: McGraw-Hill), 1967.

Penalosa, F. "The Changing Mexican-American in Southern California," Sociology and Social Research, Vol. 51, No. 4, 1967, pp. 404-417.

Peterson, W.A.; Mangen, D.S.; and Sanders, R. The Development of an Instrument Bank: Assessment of Available Instruments and Measurement Scales for the Study of Aging and the Elderly, (Kansas City: Midwest Council for Social Research), 1978.

Ragan, P.K. "Aging Among Blacks, Mexican Americans and Anglos: Problems and Possibilities of Research as Reflected in the Literature," Andrus Gerontology Center, University of Southern California, 1973.

Ragan, P.K. and Cuellar, J.B. "Response Acquiescence in Surveys: A Study of Yea-Saying Among Chicanos and Anglos," A Paper presented for the Pacific Chapter of the American Association for Public Research, 1975.

Ragan, P.K. and Simonia, M. Community Survey Report, Andrus Gerontology Center, University of Southern California, Los Angeles, CA., 1977.

Rainwater, L. and Yancy, W. The Moynihan Report and the Politics of Controversy, (Cambridge, Mass.: The MIT Press), 1967.

Reynolds, D.K. and Kalish, R.A. "Anticipation of Futurity as a Function of Ethnicity and Age," Journal of Gerontology, Vol. 29, No. 2, 1974, pp. 224-231.

Riley, M.W.; Johnson, M.; and Foner, A. Aging and Society, Vol. III, (New York: Russell Sage), 1972.

Sanchez, P. "The Spanish Heritage Elderly," in Minority Aging: Institute on Minority Aging Proceedings, Stanford, E.P. (ed.), (San Diego, CA.: Campanile Press), 1974, pp. 28-33.

Seiber, S.D. "The Integration of Fieldwork and Survey Methods," American Journal of Sociology, Vol. 78, No. 6, 1973, pp. 1335-1359.

Simonia, M.; McConnell, S.; and Newquist, D. Retirement Factsheet, Andrus Gerontology Center, University of Southern California, Los Angeles, CA., 1978.

Solis, F. "Cultural Factors in Programming of Services for Spanish-Speaking Elderly," in The National Conference on the Spanish-Speaking Eldery, Hernandez, A. and Mendoza, J. (eds.), (Kansas City: National Chicano Social Planning Council), 1975.

Sotomayor, M. "Mexican American Interaction with Social Systems," Social Casework, Vol. 52, No. 5, 1971, pp. 316-324.

Sotomayor, M. A Study of Chicano Grandparents in an Urban Barrio, unpublished Doctoral Dissertation, School of Social Work, University of Denver, Denver, Colorado, 1973.

Sotomayor, M. "Social Change and the Spanish-Speaking Elderly," in The National Conference on the Spanish-Speaking Elderly, Hernandez, A. and Mendoza, J. (eds.), (Kansas City: National Chicano Social Planning Council), 1975.

Staples, R. Introduction to Black Sociology, (New York: McGraw-Hill), 1976.

Szapocznik, J.; Faletti, M.V.; and Scopetta, M. "Psychological-Social Issues of Cuban Elders in Miami," Spanish Family Guidance Center and Institute for the Study of Aging, University of Miami, Coral Gables, Florida, 1977.

Szapocznik, J., et al. "Theory and Measurement of Acculturation," Interamerican Journal of Psychology, Vol. 12, No. 2, 1978, pp. 113-130.

Szapocznik, J. and Kurtines, W. "Acculturation, Biculturalism, and Adjustments Among Cuban Americans," in Acculturation: Theory, Models, and Some New Findings, Padilla, A. (ed.), (Boulder, Colorado: Westview Press), 1980, pp. 139-159.

Ten Houten, W.; Stern, J.; and Ten Houten, D. "Political Leadership in Poor Communities: Applications of Two Sampling Methodologies," in Race, Change, and Urban Society, Vol. 5 of Urban Affairs Annual Reviews, Orleans, P. and Ellis, W.R. (eds.), (Beverly Hills, CA.: Sage Publications), 1971, pp. 215-254.

Torres-Gil, F.M. The Political Participation of the Mexican-American Elderly, Florence Heller School of Social Welfare, unpublished Doctoral Dissertation, Brandeis University, Waltham, Mass., 1976.

Torres-Gil, F.M.; Newquist, D.; and Simonia, M. Housing: The Diverse Aged, Andrus Gerontology Center, University of Southern California, Los Angeles,, CA., 1977.

Torres-Gil, F.M. and Becerra, R.M. "The Political Behavior of the Mexican-American Elderly," The Gerontologist, Vol. 17, No. 5, 1977, pp. 392-399.

Trimble, J.E. "The Sojourner in the American Indian Community," Journal of Social Issues, Vol. 33, No. 4, 1977, pp. 159-174.

University of Southern California. "Survey of Elderly in Los Angeles County," Andrus Gerontology Center, 1977.

U.S. Bureau of the Census. Current Population Reports: Persons of Spanish Origin in the United States: March 1978, Series P-20, No. 339, Washington, D.C., USGPO, June 1979.

U.S. Senate, Special Committee on Aging. Elderly Cubans in Exile: A Working Paper, Washington, D.C., USGPO, 1971.

Valle, R. and Mendoza, L. The Elder Latino, (San Diego, CA.: The Campanile Press), 1978.

Velez, C.; Verdugo, R.; and Nunez, F. "Politics and Mental Health Among Elderly Mexican Americans," in Chicano Aging and Mental Health, Miranda, M. and Ruiz, R.A. (eds.), Washington, D.C., NIMH, USDHHS, 81-952, pp. 118-155.

Warwick, D.P. and Osherson, S. (eds.). Comparative Research Methods, (Inglewood Cliffs, N.J.: Prentice-Hall), 1973.

Weiss, C.H. "Survey Researchers and Minority Communities," The Journal of Social Issues, Vol. 33, No. 4, 1977, pp. 20-35.

143

Werner, C. and Campbell, D. "Translating, Working through Interpreters and the Problem of Perceiving," in A Handbook of Methods in Cultural Anthropology, (New York: American Museum of Natural History), 1970.

Yin, R.L. Race, Creed, Color or National Origin: A Reader on Racial and Ethnic Identities in American Society, (Itasca, Ill.: F.E. Peacock), 1973.